THE MODERN LURCHER

THE MODERN LURCHER

Michael Shaw

THE BOYDELL PRESS

© Michael Shaw 1984
Photographs © David Hancock 1984

Published by the Boydell Press
an imprint of Boydell & Brewer Ltd
PO Box 9 · Woodbridge · Suffolk IP12 3DF

ISBN 0 85115 408 5

I dedicate this book to David Brian Plummer
who not only helped my research, taught me
to put a book together, but turned over his
entire set of diaries for my perusal.

M. Shaw

Phototypeset by Galleon Photosetting, Ipswich
Printed by St Edmundsbury Press, Bury St Edmunds, Suffolk

CONTENTS

'Hope', a coursing greyhound: the starting point for most lurchers

Introduction

So, after having perused the numerous ads in sporting papers, you've decided to buy a lurcher. But before you part with your money, ask yourself one simple question: 'Is a lurcher what you really want for the job you have in mind?' What do you really want of this dog? If you want a dog simply to run hare, hare you have walked up with a dog on a slip flushed by your own devices, given sufficient law to give the hare a sporting chance and then coursed, then my advice to you would be that a lurcher is not the dog that you want. If all the reader wants is a coursing dog, then go and visit a breeder of good class greyhounds of a strain which wins well in coursing meets. Purchase a puppy from him, and train it to the highest standard of obedience one can expect from a greyhound (and greyhounds *can* be trained, believe me); break it to sheep, cattle, pigs and above all cats, put in maybe twenty miles walking a day once the dog has become a sapling hound, and then run it on hare regularly. You will then have a hare catching dog which will 'dust' any hybrid lurcher or long dog ever born and one which will win you any number of the rather pointless 'I'll run you best of three' hare catching contests. True, the dog will not be a lurcher, but then greyhounds have been bred for thousands of years to catch hares under these circumstances and as a result of this selective breeding, coursing greyhound litters rarely produce failure dogs, dogs which simply won't course or pick up their hares.

Perhaps hare coursing is not the sort of thing you want from your potential purchase and instead you'd like a dog which will be glamorous and elegant enough to win in any one of the numerous lurcher shows staged at 'hunts' or gymkhanas around the country. Don't be ashamed of wanting to own a showdog rather than a working or coursing dog. If many exhibitors of winning animals were to tell the truth, they'd admit that quite a few of their dogs have seldom seen a hare or rabbit and are kept only for the shows. Is this the sort of dog you require? Well, nothing is easier to obtain. Quite simply, find an elegant show bred greyhound bitch and mate her to an equally elegant deerhound dog, keeping the smallest puppy from the litter, as some of the puppies will grow into whoppers, 30-inch giants which are too big to win at most lurcher shows. The mating of these two elegant sight hounds will almost certainly produce a striking looking dog, with the qualities one requires in a dog destined to be a winner at a lurcher show. One small point – it won't be a real lurcher, but it will win lurcher shows well enough, of that you can be certain.

But shows aren't your scene, and you've no desire to walk up and course hares; so perhaps you want to own a dog which will win one of the lurcher races staged by most lurcher show committees and particularly by the newly formed National Lurcher Racing Club, an enthusiastic band of people who are out to produce champion lurcher racing dogs, animals capable of winning hectic two or three hundred yard dashes after a dummy hare. It's great fun, it doesn't offend members of the League Against Cruel Sports and those races provide an excellent if hectic day's sport with little of the animosity found at the lurcher shows – after all, it is difficult to dispute a judge's decision when a lurcher passes the finishing line yards in front of the other contestants. So this is the sport for you, and you require a dog capable of winning these races? Well, once again, don't waste your money on a lurcher. Go to a breeder of good track greyhounds and ask him not to tattoo the inside of its ears, or register this dog with the National Greyhound Racing Association. Rear the puppy properly; enter it to the rag in the same way one would train a whippet, and by the time the puppy is two years old it will seldom be out of the first three at lurcher racing events. It will also be indistinguishable from the majority of other 'lurchers' seen there, for in the last few years it has become the rage to mate lurchers to good track greyhounds to produce suitable dogs for lurcher racing. Yours will have a slight edge on these greyhoundy hybrids, for yours will be a 100 per cent track bred greyhound, faster than any greyhoundy hybrid ever born. If you wish to race and win on a 200-yard lurcher race, go to a breeder of racing whippets, buy an outsized dog puppy – the sort that stands head and shoulders above its brothers and sisters, betraying the fact that both its sire and dam had greyhound ancestry. Buy this puppy, and don't be too fussy about the breeder's refusal to part with the pedigree. This will be the dog to win at these sprint races, for it has been bred for generations to run similar courses and it will be streets ahead of the lurchers against which it will compete. Turn a deaf ear to the words of winners of these races who boast that their dogs have outrun greyhounds in these sprints. The greyhounds their dogs have beaten are cast dogs, damaged racers, dogs past their prime, dogs which have seen better days, but doubtless will see a lot worse, free-to-good-home dogs given a reprieve, albeit a temporary reprieve, from the canine knackers yard. A first-class track greyhound or whippet will put any racing lurcher to shame, I assure you.

2

If, however, you wish to acquire a different type of dog, a hunter, a dog capable of nosing out rabbits from cover and catching them, a dog capable of pulling down the occasional hare, taking it by stealth as much as by speed; if you require a dog to be as dextrous at taking fur as feather, as much at home knocking down a pheasant as picking up a rabbit, a country companion, the supreme hunting dog, a jack-of-all-trades, a canine Daly Thompson in fact, then look no further – the lurcher is the dog for you, and having said this, it is perhaps expedient to explain exactly what a lurcher is.

1 *What Exactly is a Lurcher?*

What exactly is a lurcher? The expression 'exactly' is certainly going to pose a few problems.

Webster's Dictionary defines a lurcher as a 'dog of nondescript breed', being something between a greyhound and a collie, and this on first sight seems to be a fair definition of the dog treasured by poachers between the two world wars. However, on examination this definition may come apart at the seams just a little. Brian Vesey-Fitzgerald, at one time editor of *The Field* travelled and lived with a variety of itinerants between the two wars and wrote copiously on the type of dog used by these northern vagrants. Vesey-Fitzgerald describes the lurcher used by these people as a blend of greyhound and Bedlington terrier, but doubles back on himself somewhat when he describes the dogs of James Arhigo, a Romany/Tinker who travelled the Welsh border country just prior to and during World War II. Arhigo's dogs were the beau ideal of the poachers dogs, fast, biddable and above all silent. Vesey-Fitzgerald rated them above a collie in intelligence, though some of Vesey-Fitzgerald's suggestions as to what constituted canine intelligence are unfortunately a little ludicrous in the light of modern researches into dog behaviour. Arhigo's dogs were breeding fairly true to type, a 23-inch broken coated brindle strain, just prior to World War II and just now and again, as proof of their ancestry, produced a collie-like puppy in some litters. It is of interest to note that Arhigo, like many pre-war lurcher trainers, only bothered to train and work bitches, and sold or destroyed any dog puppies he bred.

Of course the legendary Norfolk lurcher was the dog most writers of canine lore held in highest esteem. This dog was the product of mating a somewhat vaguely-defined dog known for some reason as the Smithfield collie (though why no-one seems to be able to explain, for drovers from as far afield as Galloway used this type of dog) a very leggy droving dog, which some believe to have been a mix of greyhound and collie, to greyhounds. This produced a fast, biddable hunting dog suitable to provide game for drovers who passed through the countryside on their way to the meat markets of the towns. I am – to say the least – a little unhappy about this story. D. B. Plummer, in his book *The Complete Lurcher* and later in *Nathan* describes the drover

4

as being a scurrilous, shiftless sort of person of the type likely to own such poaching dogs, but in fact nothing could be further from the truth. Drovers were not only entrusted with livestock for the trip to the townmarkets but they were also required to carry money on the return trip and thus the image of the poaching, shiftless drover does not ring true, I'm afraid. One curious story to illustrate the intelligence of these droving dogs is a 'must' in a book of this kind. The drives were of several hundred miles, the mixed cattle moving no further than maybe ten miles a day were common, with the stock allowed to pasture for a fee near certain inns at night – hence the great number of Half Penny Lanes found throughout Britain. However, the story has it that when the drive was over, the drover returned home in style by coach or later by train, and the dog made its way back on foot begging its way from inn to inn – a curious tale and one which makes the rather incredible 'Lassie Come Home' story a little less unbelievable.

E. G. Walsh, in his excellent and well researched *Lurchers and Longdogs* implies that he believes that this Smithfield collie, the sort described by Taplin, was an amalgam of greyhound and motley herding dogs and there is every reason to believe this to be true. Recent researches into the ancestry of the working bearded collie have revealed that when shepherds considered that their dogs were becoming a little low on the leg to work the rough terrain of the Scottish uplands they introduced the blood of deerhounds into their strains and this infusion brought about some families of bearded collie which scaled in at 27 inches at the shoulder. Thus it seems highly likely that drovers who wanted not only a bright biddable herding dog but also one with size enough to move a bad-tempered bull might also have resorted to using greyhound blood or at least some form of greyhound to breed the sort of herding dog they required.

However the majority of books on sight hounds seem to imply that the only lurchers in Britain at that time were those dogs produced along the droving routes by dint of mating these droving dogs with greyhounds; and this again is far from the truth. The Forest Charter of 1217 forbad the keeping of greyhounds by any person without permission to hunt in the Royal Forests and even made provision that any large dog kept within the forest must be maimed by striking off two of its toes, or in severe cases, of the implementation of the law, by amputating a limb to impede the wretched animal's movements. Yet there have always been poachers, men prepared to thumb their noses at legislature. Charles Trenevix Trench in his book *The Poacher and the Squire* mentions a dozen or so instances where ordinary penniless peasantry were caught hunting with greyhounds in their forests and mentions one such instance of a band of rowdies who attacked a

A modern working bearded collie

forester with staves to recover their confiscated dogs. One 'greyhound' called Collyng was renowned for its poaching prowess and caused havoc to the chief foresters of the time. Such was Collyng's sagacity that one must question as to whether this dog was strictly a greyhound and not the result of a union between a greyhound and one of the herding cur dogs which abounded in Britain at that time. Certainly the feats of cunning attributed to Collyng, described as a black greyhound, would seem to resemble the deeds perpetrated by a gypsy lurcher rather than a coursing greyhound. However there is little doubt that the greyhound which was bred prior to the seventeenth and eighteenth centuries was a great deal more biddable than our modern coursing and racing dogs; for Lord Orford, by dint of mating bulldogs to the coursing greyhounds of the day to give the breed added courage and fire, may have sacrificed intelligence in his dogs through his eugenic experiments to breed more speedy greyhounds. Perhaps, Webster's definition of the lurcher might therefore be amended to read 'a greyhound based dog blended with another breed or breeds to produce a good all-round hunting dog' – and an all-round hunting dog should be the definition of any real lurcher. This, however brings us to the highly controversial matter as to whether many of the lurchers advertised in sporting papers are strictly lurchers and not simply longdogs.

Lurchers prior to World War II were simply pot-filling dogs owned by countrymen, farmer workers and itinerants. These dogs were as at home hunting fur as feather, as keen to pick up rabbits and hares as they were to knock down pheasants and partridge. They were the ideal dog for the farm labourer poised on the breadline, and many families were fed on the catches of these lurchers. This can be best illustrated by the tale told to me by 95-year-old Richard Simpkiss, a retired bank manager who grew up in the Forest of Dean in the early part of this century.

When I was eight or nine my father worked for a Mr Lauder as a ploughman and general farm worker earning maybe 25/- a week and a cottage thrown in with the wage. There were many worse off than my father by a damn sight, but we were a large family and there were no family allowances in those days. One day father came home with a black and white lurcher bitch puppy called Peg, much to the dismay of my mother who said in no uncertain terms that there were already too many mouths to feed, and a dog was the very last thing our family needed. However, we kept the bitch who looked as much like a Welsh collie as a lurcher and we had no cause to complain about the extra mouth we had to feed. She became father's dog and only father's dog, loyal only to him and decidedly snappy with strangers, and most intolerant with children. Father took her everywhere with him and they became inseparable companions. When father ploughed she followed behind the horses and was at his heels whenever he worked around Mr Lauder's estate. Seldom did a day go by when father did not bring at least a brace of rabbits home in the evenings and frequently a hare or so joined the coneys in the pot. Mr Lauder apparently shot the land for partridge and pheasant, but turned a blind eye to my father's antics simply because as a family we had a reputation for honesty and hard work, and primarily because my older brother Thomas Simpkiss (who also worked for Mr Lauder) was unbeaten as a competitive ploughman and was an expert in breaking the Shire Horses which were Mr Lauder's pride and joy. Sometime between my ninth and tenth birthday my family decided that as I was the youngest child and suffered from asthma I should be sent to grammar school in Gloucester and an all-out effort was made to finance this venture. The whole family contributed to this enterprise and father made a business transaction with a poulterer and butcher in Stroud to provide him with saleable rabbits and hares. Thus it might be said that though I would never consider keeping a lurcher, I owe the cost of my education to the efforts of such a dog. I have no knowledge as to what happened to the dog, but I am fairly convinced that so great was the reputation of the lurcher as a catcher of rabbits and hares that the ownership of such a dog would have ensured that no farmer in the Forest of Dean area would have considered employing my father.

This then was the type of lurcher beloved by the author of *I Walked By Night*, the cur revered by Brian Vesey-Fitzgerald. But if such a dog did exist, whatever happened to it? It was a far cry from the dogs seen paraded around the show grounds by modern lurcher owners, to be traded for beer money and disposed of in a cavalier fashion whenever their owners tired of them. Something changed the lurcher of old, making it a far cry from the pot-hunting intelligent brute of yesteryear and to explain this metamorphosis I can do no better than to quote from an article by D. B. Plummer in *Shooting Times* (July 15 1982):

> The wartime years or to be more accurate the post war prosperity destroyed this breed of dog, however.
> The cessation of World War II brought a new if somewhat transient prosperity to the farmworker while the scrap metal worker and their itinerant gatherers often became rich at a time when swords were literally being hammered into plough shares. It was this change in the financial status of the traditional owners of the lurcher which brought about the metamorphosis and some consider the ruination of the breed. No longer was the supplier of filched game to feed a breadline family desired, so the original strains were adulterated with alien breeds to produce dogs capable of winning best of three hare coursing contests, feats more suitable to the powers of a coursing greyhound than a lurcher. Deerhound blood was crossed with the old fashioned lurcher to produce tall, elegant, rough coated beauties, dogs capable of coming up on a fleeing hare, but completely lacking in sagacity. Salukis, the most intractable of dogs, were added to the strains supposedly to give the new lurcher stamina, while massive infusions of greyhound blood were mingled with the now brainless mix to produce a faster, but still more brainless coursing dog.

Whether or not the lurcher of the past was superior to the modern lurcher will be questioned by many, but the purpose of this book is to

An old print of a Smithfield type droving dog

outline the qualities of the present-day lurcher rather than to dwell in the past, reminiscing on antiquities, so in the succeeding pages the writer will endeavour to describe the lurchers which are readily available today.

2 Of the Differences between Lurchers and Longdogs

E. G. Walsh in *Lurchers and Longdogs* makes a distinction between the lurcher and the longdog, whereas D. B. Plummer in his *Complete Lurcher* is inclined to lump both types together. Basically, the difference between a lurcher and a longdog is that a lurcher is the result of a sighthound, i.e. a greyhound, whippet, Saluki, deerhound, or even Afghan hound blended with another type of dog to produce a hybrid which has qualities in which the sighthound is said to be deficient – i.e. stamina, brainpower, nose and tractability. A longdog, however, is by definition a cross between two or more sighthounds to produce a coursing dog, which is purported by some coursing enthusiasts to be superior as a hare-catching dog to a pure-bred coursing greyhound. Coursing greyhound enthusiasts, on the other hand, hotly dispute the statement that longdogs make better coursing machines than greyhounds and there is some justification for their comments. Thus an *Exchange and Mart* advertisement which reads 'Lurcher puppies for sale sire Deerhound/Greyhound dam Saluki/Whippet' is not strictly speaking a lurcher; but an advert which reads 'sire Deerhound/Greyhound dam Saluki/Collie/Whippet' would by definition be a lurcher in spite of the fact that such a hybrid would have a mere one-eighth part collie in its make up, which frankly would make it only slightly more useful than a pure-bred greyhound as a hunting dog. Hence it is understandable why D. B. Plummer is keen to lump both longdogs and lurchers together; yet from the point of view of nomenclature it is expedient to use E. G. Walsh's classification and keep the two types separate when describing them.

But first a word of advice concerning the advertisements for lurchers and longdogs seen in sporting papers. The majority of these pedigrees are spurious, educated guesswork perhaps, but nevertheless guesswork. True, there are a few breeders who specialise in producing particular crosses for coursing, lamping, and hunting enthusiasts; and there are places where one can go to get a genuine deerhound/greyhound or collie/greyhound or Bedlington/greyhound hybrid, but in the majority of lurcher adverts the owners of the dogs offered for sale are simply making up pedigrees for their puppies. I spoke to one lurcher breeder who lives near Burton-on-Trent about the advertisement he sent in to two sporting periodicals, and he replied that when deerhound/greyhound hybrids were in vogue, he sold his puppies as deerhound/greyhounds; when the fashion changed, so did his adverts. The dogs offered for sale are not a whit inferior for their bogus pedigrees, but such practices do lend themselves to misuse and the would-be buyer of lurchers should take great care before making a purchase and parting with his money. However offering advice as to the purchase of a lurcher is a little premature at this stage, and we need to describe the hybrids before advising on the purchase of a puppy.

3 *Longdog Hybrids*

Deerhound/Greyhound Hybrids

At the time of writing it is nearly impossible to win at a show with any lurcher which does not have at least some deerhound in its ancestry. Deerhounds are strong, elegant dogs with deep chests which house lungs which are so large as to seem out of proportion with the rest of the dog's anatomy. These qualities are frequently inherited by the deerhound's lurcher progeny and thus a large percentage of show lurchers are 'deerhound bred'. The deerhound also sports an excellent harsh coat and a thick skin which gives the dog not only excellent protection from the rips and tears put in during a day's coursing but gives the dog a good weatherproof jacket to withstand freezing temperatures and above all driving rain. A criticism levelled at some of the very beautiful silky-coated Norfolk type lurchers is that during a day's coursing or ferreting, or a night's lamping the coat becomes a sodden mess, a mat of wet hair, mud and whatever herbage that decides to cling to the fur. Deerhound greyhound hybrids rarely sport a soft coat and while a percentage of the longdogs bred from such a mating will have thick smooth coats the majority will be either broken coated or have a hard rough coat which shakes off water and mud in a trice. Thus it is easy to see why a line up of winners at any large lurcher show usually has a fair percentage of deerhound/greyhounds in it.

However, neither the longdog nor the lurcher was intended to be a brushed and combed 'bench dog', for the real place for a running dog of any sort is not on a showground but 'in the field', and here the hybrid tends to be just a little lacking.

Frank Sheardown, the popular *Shooting Times* writer, and former African big game hunter, who now works as a freelance surveyor in East Anglia, can claim to be an authority on this hybrid. Sheardown began breeding these long dogs shortly after he purchased a small deerhound bitch from a breeder who supposedly specialised in producing dogs which would, given the chance, course hare and larger quarry. Of the bitch, Sheardown says that while she was a trier, an animal who was keen to come to terms with her quarry, she was very

13

inept at picking up a hare when she came up on it. Retrieving was also learned only after some difficulty. Sheardown had originally intended to breed a litter of pure-bred deerhounds from her, but a visit to Crufts convinced him that such a breeding programme would be of no value in the production of hunting dogs. Sheardown states that, in spite of breed publicity to the contrary, few exhibitors had actually coursed their deerhounds and worse still, several of the dogs had decidedly unsound limbs, with many exhibits sporting pins in their legs which indicated that their bones had been shattered by accidents while at exercise. In 1948 Anastasia Noble, in an attempt to put right faults which were manifesting themselves in the deerhound due to injudicious inbreeding, introduced coursing greyhound blood to improve type and structure in her dogs, but no-one used the fourth generation pure deerhounds derived from this cross.

Frank Sheardown decided not to breed pure-bred deerhounds but to breed a litter of hybrids using a collie or greyhound stud dog on his deerhound bitch. His first attempt at breeding came about when he decided to mate his deerhound bitch to a local track greyhound, a dog which had notched up a fair record on the track and was no duffer on the coursing field. Frank, however, had mixed feelings about the litter. While the puppies trained somewhat better than their coursing deerhound mother, a quality due in part to a phenomenon known as hybrid vigour, they could not be described as great coursing dogs and were certainly not as biddable as Frank would have liked them to be.

Another criticism levied at this longdog is that the first cross deerhound/greyhound males are invariably too big for coursing. E. G. Walsh, who judged Lowther Lurcher Show in 1983, stated in a letter to *Shooting News* that the exhibits in the large lurcher class were invariably deerhound/greyhound hybrids and the majority of these were ungainly oversized dogs bred from poor greyhounds and very badly proportioned deerhounds. Thus it can be stated that while the majority of winners at lurcher shows are deerhound bred, many of the very worst specimens – incongruous brutes neither elegant nor useful – also come about from this breeding.

Many breeders make somewhat outlandish claims for this cross as lamp dogs, but I'm afraid such claims must be treated with much scepticism. The deep chests of this cross allow them to run well, and it is also supposed that such a thorax produces a dog with great stamina, but the game of lamping requires not only stamina and power but an agile, nimble, dog capable of 'coming off' a fence unharmed, of twisting and turning and picking up its prey in the beam; and a large dog such as deerhound/greyhound hybrid is at a decided disadvantage at such a sport. Admittedly, few first crosses

An agile, nimble dog

A Norfolk-type lurcher

have much nose, so the tendency to run on and hunt up after the rabbit or hare has been lost in the beam is minimised; and this is a serious fault in any lamping dog. But even the dog with the best nose in the world can be whistled off a scent if sufficient emphasis is put on its early training.

Frankly, whatever the exaggerated claims made of this type of longdog, few deerhound greyhound hybrids can hold a candle to a good coursing greyhound in the coursing field. It is argued that the hybrid has greater endurance and a lot more stamina to perform arduous course after arduous course, and also greater size to facilitate it coming up on its quarry, but a well-bred coursing greyhound taken as a puppy, subjected to meticulous training for retrieving and general obedience, and given the same sort of stamina conditioning described by 'Stonehenge' (twenty miles a day behind a horse) would give a far better account of itself in the coursing field than any deerhound/greyhound longdog.

4 *The Saluki/Greyhound Longdog*

Now here is perhaps the most controversial longdog hybrid imaginable. Opinions regarding its value and worth are legion. Many will not countenance a lurcher with even a dash of Saluki blood in its veins while others swear by them. E. G. Walsh in a *Shooting Times* article of 1980 describes them as suitable only for a 'spot of disorganized coursing on Salisbury plain', but the majority of coursing enthusiasts in that area keep only Saluki/greyhound hybrids and are apparently well satisfied with them.

Salukis are desert greyhounds bred to run hare over great distances and over a very varied terrain varying from soft fine sandy dunes to rocky yardang where the fragments of stone are so sharp that they cut like knives. Salukis are therefore great athletes but are certainly not renowned for their obedience. A Saluki coursing meet is, of necessity, a disorganized affair, not because the breed enthusiasts, who stage such meets, are themselves bad organizers, but simply because the Saluki will not respond to instant command and return after a course. A degree of chaos therefore pervades the atmosphere of such meets, and, while it must be admitted that Salukis acquit themselves very well against a hare it is obvious even to the untutored by-stander that the Saluki owners have no real control over their wards and that Salukis respond to commands with a maddening slowness, if at all. Salukis are easily taught jumping, and hurdle with great enthusiasm, but it is the devil's own job to get them to retrieve by any method at all. A matter of a month ago, I watched D. B. Plummer train a pig to retrieve in order to emulate the efforts of Arkwright in the training of the pointing and retrieving pig 'Slut'. In a matter of hours the pig had absorbed the training necessary to make it a competent, if not good, retriever. Yet when I interviewed Plummer in 1976 I watched him make a very unsuccessful attempt at training an imported red Saluki dog.

Why, therefore, the reader may ask, does the lurcher enthusiast bother to cross this recalcitrant dog – with a reputation for disobedience and failure to retrieve – with a greyhound to breed a longdog? The answer is that the breed has a reputation for bottomless stamina. Phil Drabble, in his highly esteemed book *Pedigree Unknown* mentions that the big problem with the Saluki, or rather the reason the dog seems to be able to run forever, is that the dog doesn't seem to try, that is to exert itself to the full, to put every last ounce of energy into one furious do or die dash, and to a certain extent Drabble is correct. Salukis are quite simply not greyhounds and not only do they not think like greyhounds, but their method of taking their quarry is also unlike that of the greyhound. Michael Lyne, in his chapter 'Hare Coursing With Salukis' in *Coursing* (published by Standfast Press) mentions that the incredible stamina of the Saluki is not due to any unique metabolic freak of the dog's muscular structure, but simply to the fact that the breed was bred to run with a graceful, flowing action and not to put in the meteoric energy-sapping burst which characterizes the coursing greyhound's style of running. Michael Lyne mentions that at one coursing meeting in Norfolk he saw a Saluki run a course of eight minutes, a feat well beyond the capability of even the very best coursing greyhound.

This legendary stamina is supposedly transmitted to its longdog hybrid when a Saluki is mated to a greyhound, but so also is the recalcitrant behaviour, the mindless facial expression and the infuriating slowness of response to commands. A true lurcher needs to be as biddable as it is perspicacious, as able to hunt by scent as by sight. Few Saluki hybrids have nose to speak of, though one pure-bred Saluki I watched at work near Bromsgrove had an incredible nose. Fewer still are the hybrids which can be trained to any degree of obedience. As a poaching lurcher, the sort of dog the man without permission can whistle to heel at a moment's notice, this type of longdog is a positive liability. Yet it has a band of devotees who never seem to waver in their fondness for the hybrid. The Stanleys, a family of coursing enthusiasts from the Home Counties, keep nothing else and do extremely well in best-of-three hare killing contests. One should ask oneself, however, if this type of contest is the legitimate work for the lurcher. Perhaps these coursing enthusiasts might be more at home with pure-bred greyhounds or better still a pure-bred Saluki.

5 *The Whippet/Greyhound Longdog*

This hybrid is seldom seen these days and much as one might peruse the columns of *Exchange and Mart*, an advertisement for this type of longdog is rarely seen. Yet, at one time this was one of the most common of the longdogs, and let it be understood, one of the most versatile and biddable and useful of the longdog crosses.

Whippets are useful little dogs, and though some are so nesh that they decline to exercise on a rough road, others are exuberant, boisterous and totally fearless. Terry Aherne, a lurcher breeder from Tamworth owns one such bitch, a frail, almost fragile and emaciated pied, the sort of dog that would apparently succumb to a puff of wind, but she is a valiant rabbiter, fearless of cover and wire, and a great rat hunter. In fact the only quality the whippet lacks to make it a top-rate all round hunter, is its lack of size and subsequent stamina. Of course some whippets take hare, the occasional hare, mind you, not hares regularly caught and killed as some whippet owners would have one believe: those hares killed are invariably taken before the hare has time to hit top gear, for over a short sharp dash not even a top-rate coursing greyhound can vie with a really good whippet. Furthermore, no dog alive has the turning ability of a whippet, the ability to turn on a sixpence and be back into top gear without seemingly altering a stride. Size, or rather lack of it, is the only factor which makes it second to the greyhound as a catcher of hares.

Hence, longdog breeders out to breed the superlative hare-catching hybrid, often bred tall whippets proven on the track or on the coursing field with good-quality coursing greyhounds, to produce the sort of dog which has whippet take-off speed and turning ability combined with the size, strength and stride of a greyhound. D. B. Plummer, in *Rogues and Running Dogs*, mentions that these hybrids were popular around Rotherham where track whippet breeders added a dash of greyhound blood to give extra zip to their under 30lb whippets; the dogs which were too large for the race track found a ready market among coursing enthusiasts. Around Gloucester and into the Cotswolds, this cross was deliberately bred in the years following World War II by warreners, poachers and professional rabbit catchers, as an all round sporting

A coursing whippet

dog, nippy enough for rabbits, fast and strong enough to take hares, and bold enough to do larger game a mischief.

Perhaps the most famous coursing whippet greyhound hybrid was Sabre, the property of John Mason of Lechdale, Gloucester, which was rated as one of the best all round hare-catchers in the country during his day. Such was the fame of this dog that some ten years after the dog's death puppies supposedly sired by this dog were offered for sale – a truly remarkable dog in every way!

Why this crossbred has fallen from favour in the lurcher/longdog fraternity is a bit of a mystery. The dog is certainly the most biddable of all the longdogs. Perhaps the reputed lack of stamina has something to do with the decline of this type of longdog, or it may be because the crossbred has a reputation for being frail and prone to injury. Stuff and nonsense, say I. The most hardy and tough little dogs I've ever owned are from this breeding, dogs which ricochet off barbed wire fences and hedges like brindled bullets and continue with the chase as if nothing has happened, dogs which would give of their best long after their muscles had said 'stop'. There is no reason for the decline in popularity of this useful little crossbred, and the right one, having a few inches on the size of a whippet and some of the muscle of a greyhound, is capable of beating most of the Saluki and deerhound longdogs in any best-of-three coursing and catching contest.

6 *True Lurchers*

Strictly speaking a lurcher is by definition a hybrid between a greyhound and some form of herding dog and therefore four types of herding dog can be used in the creation of a lurcher: the Smithfield collie, the border collie, the bearded collie and the Alsatian, which by its very name the German Shepherd qualifies it for the title herding dog.

The Border Collie/Greyhound Lurcher

Ten years ago, during the rise in popularity of the deerhound/greyhound longdog, one seldom if ever saw advertisements for this type of lurcher. The reasons were many. Most first cross border/collie greyhound lurchers are heavily built, rather shapeless dogs and first impressions invariably count in the lurcher fraternity. Few if any of these first crosses had the speed to come to terms with a hare, and, useful as they may be, few first crosses of this breeding would ever be looked at in the lurcher shows.

Today they are different and many lurcher breeders, discontented with the mongrelly dogs which purport to be lurchers, are deliberately creating new strains of lurcher by mating border collies to greyhounds. Though not even the very best of these hybrids is fast enough to make a better than average coursing dog, they make excellent biddable lamp dogs, easily taught to retrieve and willing to run until they drop. Furthermore, such a lurcher, providing it is a genuine first cross collie/greyhound, and not a mongrel lurcher with a made up pedigree, is an excellent starting point for a strain and will improve the performance of any strain of longdog or lurcher with too high a percentage of sight hound blood in its ancestry. In fact, when a strain of working lurcher becomes reluctant to retrieve, prone to that 'faraway look' type disobedience and generally slow in learning basic training, a cross with a half bred collie/greyhound is on the cards.

In recent years two noted collie/greyhound stud dogs have produced a spate of puppies which have proved not only outstanding in the coursing field, but have also developed into excellent working lurchers picking up fur and feather in wet or dry conditions, working with ferrets, lamping and long netting. Few sires have made such a mark on the lurcher breeding programme as these males though neither dog was a looker and neither produced a spate of show winners.

The first of these collie/greyhound hybrids was Terry Aherne's Rusty. Rusty was bred by Roger Hartwell of Lutterworth, Leicester and purchased as an eight-week-old puppy by Aherne. Hartwell had produced a mastiff sized first cross collie greyhound by mating a first class collie, a Crufts obedience class winner, Traverne Taff, to a greyhound bitch of track breeding called Mandy selected because of her staying power and breeding. Rusty was an outstanding all round lurcher, a little too heavy for hare perhaps but an excellent lamp dog, a grand ferreting companion with a first class nose. Rusty was incredibly soft mouthed and rarely damaged a rabbit, let alone killed one, and this quality was passed on to his progeny. Aherne had Rusty at public stud for some two and a half years, allowing him to mate greyhounds and even lurchers and long dogs of dubious breeding. During his spell at stud he produced some eighty-four puppies but his stud career was terminated by an attack of meningitis which killed the dog in a matter of days. Such was the merit of this sire that numerous adverts in sporting papers have indicated that several enthusiasts are trying to line breed to this useful dog. The impact this dog made on the pedigrees of working and coursing lurchers can only be described as enormous.

The second collie/greyhound stud dog worthy of note is of course D. B. Plummer's Merle, a dog of dubious temperament, over-sensitive by many standards, and reluctant to tolerate the attentions of other dogs as he grew older. Breeding wise he was no great shakes, perhaps being sired by a track greyhound, a son of One and Only, out of a trial bred merle collie bitch. As a catch dog he was apt to be a trifle hard mouthed and sensitive to any form of rebuke let alone chastisement. His redeeming feature was his nose and incredible thrust when at quarry. For nose, he was perhaps inferior to Aherne's Rusty, but he was certainly a faster dog, though during his life he took but one hare and that by accident. Merle was a tenacious dog reluctant to give up a chase and this quality he passed on to his progeny.

His use at stud was restricted to greyhounds and greyhounds owned only by close friends of his owner. Even so, to date he had bred over 250 puppies and made an incredible impact on the lurcher scene. Five years ago a merle lurcher was a novelty and attracted a great deal of attention at a show. Today they are so common as to pass without notice. However, much of his success as a producer of top grade lurchers, both coursing dogs and working lurchers was due to the fact

A merle border collie, frequently used in lurcher breeding

'Rusty', a first class first cross collie lurcher

that all the bitches this dog mated were from first rate coursing stock, bitches which had excelled on the field, many of them from the Minnesota line of coursing greyhound. Some of the males he produced were excellent in shape and constitution, but some of the bitches produced by this dog were rather frail whippety creatures which were reputed to have excellent thrust even though their conformation did not inspire confidence. David Hancock of Sutton Coldfield, Britain's foremost collie lurcher authority, states that bitches he sent abroad (one to American huntress Theodora Moritz) became excellent coursers of cotton tails and jack rabbits and did more than their share of catches of raccoon.

Breeders of first cross collie/greyhounds can rarely claim that their puppies become the all-round lurcher, as much at home lamping as snapping up hares in legitimate coursing meets, but all their first crosses seem to lack is speed. Additional greyhound blood brought in by mating a first cross collie greyhound to a good quality greyhound gives the desired speed. These three-quarter bred dogs have speed enough for any quarry and 'nose and savvy' enough to be good all rounders. Furthermore these dogs have a great reputation for stamina and are usually well up in front in competitive coursing meets. Few have reach of neck enough to win at the lurcher shows where even classes for supposed collie lurchers are won by an odd mixture of sight hounds some of which resemble Salukis as much as true lurchers.

Recent convictions for deer poaching, made much of in the national press, revealed that all the dogs used for the outrage proved or purported to be collie/greyhound/greyhound crosses. Sadly, quite a few of these useful all round lurchers are being prostituted by unscrupulous lurcher men to rustle and kill sheep. If this cross bred has a fault (and all breeds of dog have their vices) it is that these lurchers have to be broken to sheep while young and broken thoroughly at that, with repeated refresher courses for any dog who displays the slightest interest in sheep or allied livestock. David Hancock states that he keeps sheep and allows his lurchers to run among them as soon as the puppies are inoculated. Hancock is fortunate that he has land and stock suitable for this purpose. For the majority of the lurcher fraternity the 'sheep breaking' of these three-quarter bred collie greyhound hybrids is an uphill struggle and frequent contact with sheep seems to be the only way to break these dogs and ensure they stay on their legitimate quarry during a course.

Three outstanding examples of these three-quarter bred collie greyhound lurchers come to mind at the time of writing. The first is Kerry, a red prick-eared, heavily muscled bitch bred by Robert McIver out of a track bred greyhound bitch and Aherne's Rusty.

Kerry, trained and worked by Aherne, has proved to be a first class all-round lurcher, a little too prone to injury to suit some, but a trier of the first order, an excellent retriever, a grand catch dog, a superb jumper and a top rate lamping dog with enough collie blood to be canny and with speed to spare.

The second and third examples are litter brothers, both of which have excelled themselves in the field – namely Eddie Jones of Wolverhampton's Celt and Alan Hooten of Doncaster's Blue. These dogs, sired by Merle, have won a terrific reputation for themselves throughout the country; though to some they appear to be a trifle heavy, their shape is deceptive for both have an extraordinary burst of speed and great stamina. Hooten's dog has numerous wins in shows, which is unusual, for a pied lurcher does not find favour among lurcher judges. Celt has to my knowledge not been placed at a show, but both have wins in obedience testing, jumping agility and speed events. Hooten's dog has also raced at flapping tracks and had some success against greyhounds, though obviously the standard of grey-hound which can be bested by a lurcher is of a rather low level. Much of the quality of these two outstanding athletes must of course be attributed to the dam side of the litter a fawn 28-inch greyhound bitch, superbly bred to Linden Eland/Minnesota lines and rated by her owner as being perhaps one of the country's best lurcher-producing greyhounds. Put to other collie bred sires she has also produced excellent all-round lurchers; and not one of her puppies has inherited her peculiar elegant strutting gait, more reminiscent of an Italian greyhound than of a superbly bred coursing bitch.

7   The Smithfield Collie/Norfolk Lurcher

Here indeed is a controversial dog, a dog reputed by Taplin (1804) to be a mix between the lurcher and the shepherd dog with a dash of maybe Dane or Mastiff. Used by drovers, it was certainly not confined to Smithfield, but was a type of droving dog found in most parts of Britain. However droving came to an end when it became more profitable to transport cattle by train than to let them endure lengthy drives between countryside and town, and the drovers and their dogs disappeared. Joanna Russell believes the breed, as such, has ceased to exist and indeed the only person claiming to breed this variety of herding dog is Aubrey Fryer of Cambridge, Gloucester. Fryer claims that his family have bred these dogs for a number of years, the original stock having come from a butcher/drover. Fryer mates these dogs to greyhounds to produce what is known as the Norfolk lurcher, some of which are curious looking dogs with a decidedly otterhoundy look about them. Fryer's Smithfield type collies are heavily coated and born blue black in colour; they have a reputation for being fiercely possessive and bad fighters when upset, with a low tolerance for any other breed of dog. The Norfolk type lurchers produced by Fryer have a good reputation in the field both as coursers and also working lurchers. They rarely top 25 inches at the shoulder and are the ideal size for all-round work.

Norfolk type lurchers, not necessarily derived from the Smithfield Collie/greyhound crosses are very popular at the time of writing. Most are silky coated dogs, pale straw or nearly white in colour of medium height and are a far cry from the deerhound/greyhound hybrids. Perhaps the most important Norfolk type dam in recent years – for the Norfolk is a type rather than a breed – is the bitch Rust, bred by Mick Douglas of Norfolk, a dropped pasterned, rather unsightly bitch, a lurcher whom no show judge would have ever considered placing, but as a coursing lurcher she would certainly take some beating. Douglas had opted out of the rat race and bought a smallholding in the wilds of Norfolk, a spot with neither running water nor electricity and here he set out to breed a superlative type of coursing lurcher of an ideal size, type and temperament for Norfolk hare coursing using the bitch Rust as a starting point and mating her and her progeny to any dog which was winning well at the 'best-of-three' hare coursing contests in the marshes. Douglas' dogs are quite a variable bunch in appearance, some being extraordinarily elegant silky coated beauties while others are merely broken-coated deerhoundy dogs. However, Douglas has an excellent reputation for producing good quality Norfolk type lurchers with both speed and bottle when up against hare, fox or deer.

Another prolific and important size of Norfolk type lurchers was Mick White's Lucky, an elegant dog, a great show winner and a valuable sire of both show and working lurchers. E. G. Walsh, who used Lucky on his bitch Tarn, was told that Lucky was a cross between a deerhound and a bearded collie, though the breeding of Lucky is questioned by many, and certainly, his two daughters from Walsh's Tarn have a decidedly bearded collie coat and demeanour. Walsh considered Lucky to be a very useful dog, not fast but with great stamina: no hedge was too large for this dog to leap, qualities which he apparently passed on to his progeny: both the puppies in question have distinguished records in the coursing field and both have won at least one championship at shows.

8   *The Bearded Collie Lurcher**

Literally reams have been written on the sagacity, hunting ability and all-round usefulness of the border collie/greyhound hybrid. Indeed, during the last few years, special classes for collie lurchers have been staged at shows in the midlands and south of England. Strangely enough, there has been little written on the bearded collie/greyhound hybrid, and I say strangely for, if anything the bearded collie is a far more suitable breed on which to base one's strain of lurcher than its border collie relative.

Bearded collies have been bred and worked in Great Britain for centuries. G. O. Willison in her book *The Bearded Collie* (1971), one of the few pieces of literature relating to bearded collies, describes an incident concerning the ship of a Polish merchant Kazimier Grabski bringing grain from Gdansk and trading for sheep and wool along the cost of West Scotland in the summer of 1514. Grabski had with him a team of rough coated lowland sheepdogs which were trained to circus dog proficiency, and so impressed one of the Scottish shepherds that he traded a matched ewe and horned ram for a trio of these dogs. It is a delightful story, but it is extremely unlikely that these dogs became the ancestors of the present day bearded collies.

Almost all European countries west of Asia Minor have herding and droving dogs which closely resemble the working bearded collie. In fact many Spanish sheepdogs which work sheep and goats on the arid plateau of the Meseta are indistinguishable from the old type of bearded collie (a tan and white rangy dog) as painted by Phillip Reinagle 1749–1833, though for some reason Reinagle calls his dog an Old English Sheepdog in spite of the fact that the dog is undocked and very different from the ancestor of the present day Bobtail. Rumanian and Hungarian sheepdogs would also pass for the cur-like sheepdog called the 'Scotch Colly' in Gesse's *Anecdotes On Dogs* of 1844 (a delightful, if very anthropomorphic book). What is likely is that during the migration of the Celts in the second century BC two

---

* To consider oneself able to write a brief chapter on this type of lurcher would be vanity indeed for David Hancock, a close friend of mine, is an authority on this type of lurcher and he has kindly contributed the following pages concerning the merits and defects of the bearded collie/greyhound lurcher – *Michael Shaw*.

'Taffy', a bearded collie lurcher

distinct types of herding dog accompanied the Celts on their march across Europe to Britain: a smallish narrow-headed dog which became the ancestor of the border collie and a broader-headed larger type of dog with a distinct trace of ban dog in its make up, which was the ancestor of the present day beardie.

Bearded collies are popular today and though many breeders of the glamorous long-coated show strains of beardie boast that their dogs are only five or so generations away from the hill-working sheepdogs of the Highlands, it has to be admitted that the breed has declined considerably in intelligence and workwise during those generations of inactivity. Modern show-bred beardies are often shy and inclined to be scatty and over-exuberant – a far cry from their rock steady hill sheepdog ancestors, and totally unsuitable for breeding a first class reliable and efficient lurcher.

Genuine unadulterated strains of working bearded collie are rare at the time of writing and sadly likely to become even rarer for the increasing popularity and general availability of the border collie seems to be forcing the beardie to extinction. To secure suitable animals on which to base a strain of lurcher, the would-be breeder would need to seek out hill farmers living in remote areas of Scotland and Northumberland. One or two working beardies can be seen working sheep and cattle in the midlands, but these seem to be kept as novelties and are rarely used for breeding. Few of the Scottish working strains breed absolutely true to type for in most litters of beardies one finds a puppy or two which is indistinguishable from a pure-bred, heavy coated, border collie. Yet though these working beardies lack the glamorous hirsute look of their show bred cousins, the intelligence, vigour, stamina and general tractability of the working-bearded collie is equal to that of the border collie. Indeed, many would be capable of competing in the working sheepdog tests which are now so popular on television.

Curiously, specimens of bearded collie which appear in mixed border/beardie litters are invariably taller than their border collie type siblings. Logan, an authority on the bearded collie, believes that in certain hilly and rocky areas of Scotland deerhounds were crossed into the strains of beardie to breed a taller, leggier dog more capable of working the steep terrain. At the turn of the century, when bearded collies were as numerous as border collies in Scotland, it was not uncommon to find a twenty-seven inch male working sheep in certain glens. Furthermore the beardie is usually longer in the stifle than the border and it passes on this as well as its extra height to its lurcher offspring when mated to greyhounds and other sight hounds.

First cross border collie/greyhound lurchers are useful all round hunting dogs, ideal for rabbiting working cover and lamping, but most are a trifle too cloddy with too much substance and not enough leg to be first class hare coursing dogs. D. B. Plummer in his book *The Complete Lurcher* states that when a first cross collie/greyhound is a greyhoundy shape the result is a world beater, but such a specimen is rare, and less than 0.5 per cent of first crosses are first class hare coursing dogs, though in all fairness one should add that most collie greyhounds are capable of picking up the occasional hare if the slip is not too long and the terrain is not too unsuitable.

Bearded collies are slightly taller than borders and, in spite of their heavy coats, quite finely built and athletic. These qualities are passed on to their lurcher offspring, so many of the first crosses between greyhound and beardie are lightly built enough to take hare on long and arduous courses, for collie stamina is legendary. The average

31

bearded collie/greyhound is in fact a full inch taller than its border collie counterpart and this height difference gives it a decided edge as a hare catcher.

Border collie/greyhound first crosses are usually a little unsightly and mongrelly and the short thin coat does little to disguise its cloddy shape. Bearded collie/greyhound hybrids are invariably rough or broken coated, with coats ranging from those sported by Afghan hounds to Bedlington terriers, and smooth coated puppies are an exception in any litter. Aesthetics apart, the coat is thick, wiry, weatherproof and an excellent protection against thorns and nettles.

Most bearded hybrids are remarkably level and homogeneous and resemble the true breeding lurcher types one finds on the camp sites of Spanish and Portuguese Chalo gypsies. Indeed many cynologists believe that just as the legendary Norfolk lurcher was the result of infusing greyhounds with the blood of droving dogs, so the lurcher types found in the Iberian peninsula are probably the result of repeated crosses twixt sight hounds and Spanish herding dogs.

Thus it is the writer's contention that the beardie rather than the border collie is the ideal start for an all-round lurcher. What is surprising, however, is that no-one has considered producing a true breeding strain of lurcher from the bearded collie/greyhound hybrids.

9 *The Alsatian Greyhound Lurcher*

Aubrey Fryer in a letter to *Shooting News* in September 1983 concerning this cross-bred states that an Alsatian/greyhound is not strictly a lurcher, but simply a mongrel, as by definition a lurcher is a hybrid between a greyhound and a shepherd dog. Reluctant as I am to oppose such an authority, I'm afraid Aubrey is quite wrong. Firstly, the term Alsatian is a misnomer, for the dog is not a native of Alsace and the name was given to the dog because of anti-German feeling during World War I, the same ridiculous racial prejudice that inspired bands of unthinking louts to take out their spleen on dachshunds because of the breed's Teutonic connections. The real name for the Alsatian, a name which the British have adopted during the last decade or so, is *Deutsche Schaeferhund* which means 'German Shepherd Dog', and while few Alsatians are used for herding work in Great Britain several German reports show marked herding ability. In fact trials are staged in Germany each year to test and possibly to exploit the natural herding instinct of this very useful breed, and dogs considered worthy of the name of German Shepherd dog are awarded the title HGH an abbreviation for *Herdengebrauchshund* which means quite simply herding dog. Thus, strictly speaking, an Alsatian/greyhound cross does qualify for the title a true lurcher.

In recent months the Alsatian/greyhound hybrid has received a great deal of publicity concerning its merits and failings as a lurcher. Firstly, an appraisal of the qualities of the German Shepherd dog is called for, and frankly not even the incredible border collie can claim to be such a versatile dog. Not only are Alsatians perhaps the best guard dogs available, capable of being trained for any form of police work, but there are few other tasks an Alsatian cannot master. Many will herd sheep with some enthusiasm, not perhaps with the same delicate finesse of a border collie, but it is said the phlegmatic disposition of the Alsatian makes it a better cattle dog than any British collie. Tales of the retrieving and hunting ability of this dog are many and few dogs, scent hounds excepted, have the infallible nose of the German Shepherd Dog. Furthermore, the Alsatian has a remarkable turn of speed, a speed which is not reflected by its elegant and rather stately appearance, and while it would be ludicrous to compare the

'Bruno', an 8-month-old Alsatian greyhound lurcher

rabbiting ability of the Alsatian with that of the whippet, Alsatians make an excellent base line for lurcher breeding having pluck, intelligence, nose and a fair turn of speed.

First cross greyhound/Alsatian lurchers are all very similar and all seem to resemble a rather leggy, lightly built Alsatian. One of these dogs photographed by David Hancock for his book *Lambourn*, a dog belonging to David Boyles of South Molton, would have passed for an early 1920 pure-bred Alsatian, but having said that, these hybrids are deceptively fast and fearless. In fact it has been said that whenever a person has kept such a dog they are never content with any other variety of lurcher or longdog. It might also be a suitable time to explode a myth concerning shape and the ability of a dog to take hare. Frail, whippety lurchers, as slender as a Saluki, are usually not the world beaters one would think, and quite often heavily muscled dogs

come out best against a hare over a long and difficult course. Eddie
Jones' Celt is a good example of this type of dog: Celt is a powerfully
muscled dog resembling a half-bred collie greyhound as much as a
three-quarter bred. His prowess at hare catching is well known, yet
newcomers to coursing frequently accost Eddie and ask him if the dog
is fast enough for hare. Most lurchers are fast enough to come to terms
with a hare, but it is only at this point that the course begins, and it
requires a bright, dextrous and extremely courageous dog to stay with
a hare and catch it over a particularly lengthy course. To return
however to actual accounts of the exploits of the Alsatian/greyhound
hybrid: D. B. Plummer in *Rogues and Running Dogs* makes mention of a
notorious deer poacher from Leighton Buzzard who made havoc in
the Woburn Deer Park using an Alsatian/greyhound hybrid. Plummer
does not name the 'notorious deer poacher', but he is referring to
Geoffrey Battams, a Bedfordshire based Robin Hood figure who is
much revered by Southern lurchermen. Battams' dog Spider,
resembled a brindled Alsatian, flat-backed without angulation
perhaps, but with pricked ears and a typical Alsatian expression.
Spider's breeding will be questioned by many, but his Alsatian
ancestry becomes obvious as soon as one sees a photograph of the dog.
Battams fetched the dog from a local dog pound after a band of
itinerants had bred a litter of these hybrids, taking the dog they
considered best and simply abandoning the rest of the litter on the side
of the road. They returned to the roadside camp the next year and
apparently told Battams the breeding of the dog.

Spider became a tremendous hunting dog. Alan Hooten who
hunted with Battams at one time describes Battams as a quiet,
reticent man with an incredible link with the dog, a link that could
only have been brought about by some peculiar form of man/dog
telepathy. For all his bad publicity concerning his deerkilling exploits,
Battams has a reputation for being a first class lurcher man, the sort of
man who 'sticks with his dog' not selling it, swopping it, or giving it
away at the merest excuse or manifestation of some form of weakness
or fault in the dog. Hooten describes Spider as the best coursing dog
he has ever seen, not a particularly fast dog, but a striker supreme and
one who invariably brought down his hare. Hooten says that if a hare
got up in front of Spider, and Spider considered it too long a slip or an
unsuitable slip – too near a hedge or some other spot where a hare could
easily escape – Spider refused to go, and no amount of encouragement
from Battams could change his mind. This of course is the quality
which separates a lurcher from a longdog, a quality of perception and
discretion which is only found in lurchers with a huge percentage of
herding dog blood. Many lurcher men will not countenance a dog

which will not 'try' whenever it is slipped, but such coursing men would in point of fact be better off owning a greyhound.

Hooten says Battams actually kept a curious tally of the hares, rabbits and other prey Spider took, putting a tick for every hare caught on one wall of his bedroom and another smaller tick for rabbits. Eventually he ran out of space for the rabbit count, but on Spider's retrieving, Hooten says Spider had five hundred hare ticks to his credit.

Sufficient proof of the value Battams places on this hybrid is the fact that he has made contact with one of the Midlands top lurcher breeders to produce a good type Alsatian/greyhound hybrid and arranged to take the entire litter to distribute amongst his friends. It seems unlikely that any lurcher type could be paid a better compliment.

10 *The Bedlington Terrier/Greyhound Lurcher*

As has already been mentioned, this type of lurcher was considered by Vesey-Fitzgerald to be the original lurcher, at least among the itinerant bands who poached and coursed from Inverness to the Yorkshire borders. I have taken the liberty of listing this cross as a lurcher, and frankly I must confess to a sneaking liking for the dog. The dog looks the part of a lurcher – the type of dog at home beneath a vardo, varminty dogs with scruffy, unkempt coats and silky top knots, bulging eyes and slender, slinky shapes.

Perhaps I have been fortunate in having had a well-bred Bedlington greyhound to start my interest in lurchers; shortly after World War II there were suitable Bedlington terriers to breed good lurchers. What happened to the Bedlington terrier since then is a matter of speculation. Miss Margaret Williamson of Neath, founder of the Working Bedlington Terrier Club, believes that breeders hell-bent on producing show champion terriers regardless of their working ability, mated tiny nervous poodles to their terriers to improve their coat and movement. The result must have been devastating. At one time the Bedlington terrier was considered to be one of the gamest dogs alive, having pluck equal to that of the bull terrier, prepared to die rather than give an inch, and so aggressive that Durham gypsies, tinkers and miners used the dogs for pit fighting, much in the same way that Staffordshire nail makers used bull terriers. In fact there was probably a high percentage of bull terrier blood in the original Bedlington terrier mix. So game was the Bedlington terrier that breeders of fell terriers and also breeders of Jack Russell type terriers in Wensleydale used to mate the Bedlington to their dogs if they considered their dogs were becoming low on 'bottle'. What must a cross between this type of dog and a poodle have done for the breed!

In the 1970s, interest in the Working Bedlington terrier began to revive, partly due to the good offices of Miss Williamson and partly to George Newcombe, the Chairman of the Working Bedlington Club. Miss Williamson decided to sort out strains which had either no poodle blood or at least only a tiny percentage of this blood, and work on their blood lines to resuscitate the breed. Newcombe, however, became a little disenchanted with the idea, as he believed that the guts had long since been bred out of the terrier and no amount of careful line breeding would revive this blind and wilful courage. Thus Newcombe resolved to mate his best Bedlington terriers to the gutsiest fell terriers he could find. (In fact he used a calm sensible strain bred by John Cowan of Embleton, a strain which dated back to the dogs of Jim Fleming of Grasmere.) Newcombe's dogs are now 'fourth generation bred' and breeding relatively true to type.

Now here's the rub. The show bred strains are usually tall elegant dogs – the size of racing whippets, in fact – and a little too big to get to ground. The new type of dog bred by both Miss Williamson and George Newcombe are smaller animals, scarcely bigger than a working fell terrier, and, though these dogs usually have courage and working instinct to spare, they are scarcely big enough to provide a good sized hare coursing lurcher even when mated to a very large coursing greyhound. The show bred stock of course is large enough, but many of the strains lack the fire of the old-type Bedlington and thus tend to produce a lurcher which looks the part but lacks the 'bottle' during a hard course or contact with a thorny hedge or a fox. If one can find the right sort of Bedlington and mate it to a large coursing greyhound bitch the resultant litter could be just the ticket. They won't have collie brains – no lurcher has for that matter, but they will be bright enough to learn to retrieve well and steady enough to be broken to cattle and stock. Most lurchermen want little more from their dogs anyway.

During the last four years, the lithe agile Bedlington/greyhound has found favour with the show fraternity. At Lambourn 1981 and 1982 (sadly the last of the Lambourn Lurcher Shows for reasons I shall explain later) the majority of the winning dogs had a decided Bedlington terrier look about them, although some of the overall winners had more than a hint of the deerhound's elegance. Could it be that judges are at last waking up to what exactly constitutes a lurcher and are putting up winners which would be more at home on the field than on the Crufts show bench?

The place for the lurcher is the field and not the show ring, and it is here the Bedlington/greyhound lurcher comes into its own. My own lurchers, bred by Don Bakewell of Leicestershire are smallish dogs, by modern standards, scarcely 23 inches at the shoulder and roach-backed enough to make them an embarrassment at the shows. Both dog and bitch are remarkably soft mouthed, excellent rabbiters and for first-cross lurchers quite good on hares. Unlike D. B. Plummer, I believe the type to be docility itself and easily broken to cats, ferrets and other dogs. Mine show a reluctance to tackle fox in spite of their terrier ancestry, but two litter mates of these dogs have proven to be great fox-catching lurchers and useful at predicting when a fox will bolt. If they have faults it is that they are sharp with sheep and need frequent and quite severe correction. Neither are they the one man dogs that first cross collie lurchers are prone to be (which is perhaps a blessing in the chop and change of the lurcher world) and either dog could be easily stolen by anyone who wielded a spade or better still carried a lamp.

As lampers, many Bedlington lurchers are first-class and though it would be ludicrous to rate their stamina with that of a collie greyhound cross the Bedlington lurchers I have seen have been more than the equal of any longdog. Bedlington greyhounds are nippy, rather than possessing the dazzling burst of speed of the longdog, but nippy dogs are certainly more useful as lampers. Furthermore, unlike collie lurchers, they are not jealous retrievers, dogs which will only retrieve a rabbit to hand when there is no other dog leashed and ready to snap up their catch. Collie lurchers are absolute devils for jealous retrieving and will often pace around the lamper refusing to give up their catch while the lamper is holding another lurcher. In spite of their terrier disposition (and terriers must be the very last word as far as jealous workers are concerned) the Bedlington greyhounds I have owned and seen do not have this jealous streak, and while it has to be admitted that it is not particularly easy to train a Bedlington greyhound to retrieve, once the lesson has been taught thoroughly it usually sticks.

Bedlington lurchers need careful training if they are to be of use, however, and (because the potent blend of greyhound and terrier is apt to get on top of the newcomer to the lurcher world) they are perhaps not the best of dogs to own as your first lurcher.

As daytime lurchers they take some beating and are as keen to work cover as a spaniel. Bakewell's strain of Bedlington greyhound are a little inclined to be more disposed towards hunting fur than feather, but once the penny has dropped they will pick up a partridge or a pheasant as well as any hybrid lurcher; though in all fairness it should be pointed out that my own lurchers were twenty-seven months of age before they stopped being frightened by a pheasant exploding from cover or a partridge whirring up from stubble. Once they had caught their first game birds, however, they became enthusiastic bird hunters and now mine rank level with any type of lurcher as a pot filler.

11   *Other Crosses Used to Breed Lurchers*

An amazing variety of lurchers are advertised in *Exchange and Mart*, some with spurious pedigrees, others the result of a breeder who wishes to breed something different. From time to time some really exotic hybrids are seen. A few years ago a hybrid litter of Dobermanns and Deerhounds were advertised and one of these crossbreds is shown in David Hancock's *Lambourn*. At one time there seemed to be a spate of bull terrier/greyhounds advertised and many of the Lancashire coursing fraternity still swear by this cross as a coursing lurcher. Other crosses recorded over the last few months include blends of retrievers, poodles, Airedales, and Soft-coated Wheaten terriers with greyhounds and, while it has to be admitted that some of these crossbreds have proved excellent all round lurchers, the beginner would do well to stick with the traditional tried and trusted varieties of longdog or lurcher. I am, I admit very conservative about lurchers and consider that the dogs described in this chapter have more than stood the test of time, and that any newcomer would do well to forget about the exotic crossbreds (no matter how attractive the breeding sounds) and stick to the conventional lurchers and longdogs.

12 Small Lurchers

By small lurchers I mean dogs below 21 inches at the shoulder: I consider the conventional show standards of below 23 inches and above 23 inches are nothing short of ludicrous. So, having upset the show fraternity by this statement, may I upset the owner of the small lurcher even more by stating that for the life of me I cannot see why such dogs are bred.

The small lurcher is in no way superior to the pure-bred whippet as a pot filler and nowhere nearly as nippy or quick off the mark. It can be argued, I suppose, that whippets tear easily on cover and are supposedly a little nesh and reluctant to face thorn. To those who pass such criticism I say 'Go and watch a whippet coursing meet'. Most of the coursing whippets will try until they drop and seem to have an inexhaustible source of stamina in their fragile little bodies. I have yet to see a coursing-bred whippet which will not crash into cover after a rabbit. Whippets, particularly whippets from the very good coursing strains we produce in Britain, respond instantly to a situation and are seemingly always in a state of readiness. Small lurchers with even a dash of whippet in their ancestry are seldom as sharp as a pure-bred whippet and certainly do not have that sparkle for which a coursing whippet is renowned.

Most small lurchers are either the result of mating two very mixed types of lurcher together, when the recessive whippet genes have somehow combined to throw a small lurcher, or they are simply the misguided attempts of lurcher breeders to reduce the height of outsized deerhound bred lurchers by mating them to whippets. The results are usually unsatisfactory, though it should be pointed out that there were once some really excellent whippet/greyhounds bred in Gloucester a few years ago. More often than not, the small lurchers one sees at the shows are far too heavily loaded with flesh in proportion to height to make useful running dogs.

However there are some whippet lurchers that are deliberately bred by crossing particular sight hound breeds with whippets to breed rabbiting and ferreting dogs. The most popular cross is the Bedlington terrier/whippet hybrid and the reasons given for the production of these lurchers is that a dash of Bedlington blood will give the whippet

41

more fire and 'get up and go'. To those who wish to believe this, all I can say is 'go and see a kennel of good registered coursing whippets'. They have a sparkle which cannot be equalled and fine guts and willingness to hunt that will put the average show-bred Bedlington terrier to shame. The whippet/Bedlington hybrid may have a woolly, thorn resistant coat and look the part, but most couldn't hold a candle to a pure-bred coursing whippet for alertness and general usefulness.

Collie/whippet hybrids are also not as useful as one might imagine. A good sized greyhound can take the extra bone and substance a cross with a collie usually gives (though most first cross collie/greyhounds are usually quite hideous) but whippets have neither bone or height to take this extra substance a collie cross might confer. Some years ago I bred a litter of these crossbreds using a good quality cast whippet bitch from the Laguna strain, and a game old working collie from Blackwell. The puppies were given every chance, put out to suitable homes and trained, and entered by thinking caring dog lovers. Not one proved better than merely second rate.

Thus if the potential lurcher owner requires a small dog suitable for hunting hedges, ferreting, and a spot of general rabbiting, he would be wise to forget the small lurcher and spend his money on a puppy from a first class strain of working whippet.

13 *Buying a Lurcher*

Buying a lurcher puppy is easy these days, as lurchers are advertised in most sporting papers. Getting the right one to suit one's own temperament is a little more difficult and hence some advice seems called for.

Firstly, decide on exactly which cross you need and do not be swayed from your goal by the low cost of any unsuitable puppy offered you, the proximity of the seller to one's home or the cajoling sales talk of the seller of the puppies. Get to know exactly what you require in a lurcher, and don't settle for less. Take a tight hold on your money, and part with it only when you are absolutely certain that the puppy is what you want. It's also a point to remember that, next to used car dealers, some lurchermen are the greatest con men in the world and frequently sell awful mongrels as lurchers, producing a pair of well groomed glamorous beauties when asked to show the parents of the litter, starlets which are in no way connected with the monsters offered for sale. It's a common trick, I'm afraid, and after purchase there is nothing the buyer can do about it, apart from offering his monstrosity for sale to yet another sucker; but then there are suckers a-plenty in the lurcher world.

Most of the incredible pedigrees of lurchers offered for sale in honest-to-goodness magazines such as *Shooting Times, Shooting News,* and that bible of lurcher keeping, *Exchange and Mart* are bogus. The majority are simply made up on the spot, including in them whatever the current fancy is in the lurcher world. If deerhound crosses are popular, then you can bet the pedigree will include at least one reference to deerhounds, for example 'Sire deerhound × greyhound × Saluki/collie, Dam deerhound/greyhound × Bedlington/whippet' – a doughty mix if ever there was one. If collie crosses are in vogue the vendor quite simply strikes out the deerhound and inserts collie in the advert and if that doesn't sell the puppies then perhaps a liberal dose of Bedlington blood added to the fictitious mix will attract a buyer or so. The truth is only a small percentage of lurcher breeders have the remotest idea what the breeding of their dogs is. Most lurchers are the result of a score or more of lurcher to lurcher matings arranged by amateurs with no particular goal in mind other than to breed a litter or so of puppies. Some puppies from these unpredictable mixes will be just the ticket, perhaps; but the majority will be seond-rate, and quite a few very little use at all.

It is in fact very difficult for the newcomers to the breed to pick a good lurcher puppy, and in spite of the recent TV programme concerning gypsies and gypsy dogs there is no sure way of picking up a good puppy from a very mongrelly lurcher litter. Avoid the breeder who adds bits of Bedlington to a dash of whippet/greyhound and throws in a dash of deerhound/saluki to bring the size up. The best lurchers have very few breeds in their make up. In fact, the fewer the nunber of breeds used to create a lurcher, the better the chance of getting a really top-rate dog from that litter.

Picking out a puppy from any litter of lurchers is a very hit and miss affair. Some crosses come very true to type. Bedlington/greyhound first crosses usually produce a very level litter with little to choose between the puppies. Likewise the greyhound × collie/greyhound cross, reputed by many to be the ideal type of all-round lurcher, usually comes very true to type, resembling a rather greyhoundy lurcher with a head which is slightly broader than that of a greyhound. Personally I believe that if the parents are 'genuine' then one could literally pick out any three-quarter bred collie greyhound and come up with a winner. Half-bred collie greyhound crosses are a different kettle of fish, and it takes a wise man indeed to pick out the ideal half-bred collie lurcher from a litter of eight-week-old puppies. However, if you do come up trumps in this canine lucky dip, the result is a world beater, a dog which will make you the envy of every lurcherman for miles around. It would take a man with amazing powers of prediction to pick out the best puppy from such a litter – though you can be sure any puppy from this mating will work hedgerows and with lamp.

Of course not all lurcher to lurcher litters turn out to be a heterogeneous mess. Just now and again one sees a lurcher that is just what one wants, but before racing out and ordering a puppy from the same mating, check on what all or most of these puppies look like, and more important still, how the entire litter perform in the field; for a lurcher is (regardless of its looks) a working dog, and it is working instincts, not the looks, which count in the long run. If the rest of the litter are also working well and are roughly the same type as the one which caught your eye, then a puppy from the repeat mating may be just what you want.

Many lurcher books suggest that the place to buy a lurcher puppy is from the owner of a working lurcher bitch who decides to breed a litter of puppies with the purpose of keeping back one for himself to keep the line going. This may be the place to buy a puppy, but it would be wise to remember that few of these back street lurcher breeders have any idea of the genetic make up of their own bitches and less still of the breeding of the sire they intend to use. Another point to remember is that few of these breeders are prepared to split up a litter until the puppies are twelve weeks of age, as the object of breeding such a litter is to keep one puppy back for themselves. The chances are that the lurcher breeder will have a close friend who fancies a puppy or so, and thus by the time they have taken out the puppies they consider suitable, the choice left open to you is rather limited, to say the least.

Another great sales gimmick to lure in the sucker for fleecing is the advert which states 'Gypsy bred lurchers for sale', as if this was proof of the value of the puppies. For some reason or other, the gypsy is looked on as being the best possible dog trainer and the most skilful and successful poachers imaginable. The truth is few gypsies, tinkers or other itinerants really look after their dogs, and if you drive past any site you will quickly be convinced that this is not the place to buy a puppy. The majority of itinerants do poach, but they rely on the fact that if they get caught by the time a summons is served they are three counties away and living under another name, so don't be encouraged to buy a lurcher puppy simply because the vendor claims they are 'gypsy bred'. Battams' Spider may have been gypsy bred, but it should be remembered that it was Battams' skill as a dog trainer which made Spider the animal he was, not merely the fact that he had been bred and born on a gypsy site.

Last but certainly not least we come to the professional lurcher breeder as a source of a lurcher puppy. Here let us immediately differentiate between the professional lurcher breeder and the snapper up of 'odds and sods', cripples, blown and failed lurchers, cheap-at-the-price bargain bitches, and lurchers with funny habits which they have picked up from indifferent owners who are passing through the lurcher-owning phase in their development. This miscellany of dogs, this kaleidoscope of canine misfits, are then mated to a track greyhound or a greyhoundy hairy lurcher and the puppies sold as deerhound/greyhounds whippet/Bedlington terriers or even collie/ greyhounds – whatever is in fashion at the time. These are not professional lurcher breeders, merely dabblers in breeding puppies, puppies which will be passed on from uncaring home to uncaring home just as their parents were.

At the time of writing properly bred lurchers with genuine and authentic pedigrees are fetching a very high price – particularly collie-bred hybrids. Thus it is very profitable to breed the real genuine article, using track bred or (better still) coursing greyhound bitches, and a really good class stud dog preferably a tried and tested dog with a track record of many useful lurcher puppies to his credit. The real genuine lurcher puppy will fetch a good price and find a ready market with lurcher enthusiasts. Some of the lurcher fraternity refrain from buying from such breeders for some reason or other, possibly because many of these breeders produce puppies only to sell and make a profit. However, this attitude towards such breeders is as ridiculous as the notion of not drinking milk because the dairy which sells it is only there to make a profit. Professional breeders of note, and maybe half a dozen come to mind at the time of writing, have built up a reputation not by the usual bar room and beer tent talk, but by producing first class puppies which have done the job for a number of satisfied buyers. Check the track record of these breeders. Many keep, or rather breed, only one cross in deerhound/greyhound, collie/greyhound, or Bedlington/greyhound. Few indulge in weird and outlandish crosses like Borzoi/Dobermann for while such crosses might produce a useful puppy now and again, the majority of the lurcher fraternity would not dream of trying such a hybrid. A professional lurcher breeder will only keep a tried and tested lurcher cross, one which has stood the test of time and proved popular with the coursing and rabbiting enthusiasts.

Personally, these are the places I would go to buy a puppy, after checking around on how well a particular breeder's stock have performed. The reasons for purchasing a puppy from such a breeder are many. Firstly, the breeder is rarely interested in keeping back a puppy for himself, nor has he usually promised a pick of the litter to a friend. Hence if the would-be buyer books the puppy in advance, he can go to the breeder and have his pick of the litter. Secondly no breeder wishing to stay in business is likely to palm off a bad puppy on the buyer – for a good name is always worth more than a few pounds in pocket from the sale of a dubious puppy. These are the people to see about buying a 'genuine' first class lurcher puppy.

Lastly, it is essential to mention the 'dealer' as a source of lurcher puppies, and at the time of writing there are more dealers than professional lurcher breeders in Britain. Dealers buy in stock which breeders cannot sell and may have a hundred or so puppies, some healthy, some diseased, through their hands each year. Pedigrees are lost along the way and made up to suit the buyer on the day of the sale and there is no redress for bad or sickly puppies bought by the client. Frankly, I think there is little more to be said about buying puppies from a lurcher dealer. The would-be buyer need only read this paragraph again and make up his mind as to whether this is the place to buy any puppy of any breed.

14 *Selecting a Puppy*

Once you have decided which cross would suit you and where to buy such a puppy, and have checked the credentials of the buyer and seen some of the stock produced by him, it is time to visit the premises and choose a puppy. Before one does however there is one small hurdle to overcome. It's even money that on hearing that you are off to buy a lurcher puppy, a friend will pop round and just happen to mention that someone has a grown dog for sale – cheap. There will be a variety of reasons why this dog is for sale (and for sale very cheaply at that). Reason one is that the owner of the dog is going away and as a great number of lurcher enthusiasts are of dubious honesty the term 'going away' has special significance. Even though the dog has been exceptionally well trained, he is offering it at a very low price as he wishes to sell it quickly to a good working home. Fine – and while no one can deny that some lurchers owned by certain people who have to keep special appointments with HM Prisons are excellent dogs, be sure that the dog is all it is made out to be; and above all make absolutely certain that the crime for which a person is 'going away' is a fairly serious one meriting a particularly long sentence. Short-term offenders who sell their lurchers for a song before 'going inside' have an unfortunate knack of wanting their dogs back when they come out again, as a recent court case will verify. Another type of dog offered for sale is the seasoned lamping dog, the one who can do everything from taking fox and deer to bringing rabbits gently to hand – all at the tender age of eighteen months. (Incidentally, nearly every trained lurcher offered for sale is invariably eighteen months old, much as tinkers and didikais only sell horses which are eight or thirteen years of age.) Well, let's debunk this piece of sales gimmickry. Most lurchers only start to become useful at the age of perhaps two and a half, an age when they have learned discretion, outgrown the silly behaviour which bugs all sight hounds until their second year, and have finally decided how to sort out the bobbing and jerking of a running hare or the incredible dash for home of a lamped rabbit. What then of the eighteen-month-old genius who is offered for sale with a trial to prove its merit? Chances are he'll do fine during the trial run – if the run is not too long and too taxing. Chances are he won't do quite so well

A litter of fine bright-eyed first-cross puppies

after a hard night's lamping or an even harder day's coursing and he may even manifest a few physical peculiarities such as wheezing or toppling over after a hard course or so. Most of the 'this dog will do it all' variety offered for sale are well past their prime seven- and eight-year-olds whose owners have run them without pity (and without using a great deal of sense) and have allowed their dogs to rupture their diaphragms or strain their hearts. Such dogs are termed 'blown' in the dog-dealing trade and never completely recover, no matter how well they are treated and how long they are given to rest. One such dog, sent to the Midlands from the Isle of Man, did the rounds of maybe eight supposed lurcher enthusiasts, before being passed to one particularly insensitive dolt who ran the dog unfit and decidedly under the weather, finally causing it to keel over and die. Hence the reason why this well trained 'sapling eighteen-month-old lurcher!' is going for a song! The majority of trained dogs offered for sale have been either damaged through overwork and running unfit or have developed a nasty little habit which makes their owners want to get rid of them.

One tale comes readily to mind, of a Welsh-bred dog which was sold to a man near Bromsgrove. The buyer was also given the customary night's lamping as a trial. The dog was a beauty, an eye-catching steel grey and white collie marked lurcher with just enough deerhound blood to give it height and a roughish coat. I went over the dog for the would-be buyer, and though one toe seemed just a little weak, otherwise it was a cracker with lung space to spare, muscle to carry it through the hardest day's coursing and enough breadth between the eyes to show the beast was not too close to the sight hound and thus reasonably easy to train. So far, so good; and I advised the buyer to ask the seller for a night's trial before buying, as the purchase price for such a beauty was a mere £60, a mere bagatelle for a dog of this conformation.

At all events the dog ran well, caught well and retrieved to hand like a spaniel; and to cut a long story short my associate bought him. Next night he tried the dog again, and had the misfortune to run the dog on land where cattle and sheep were pastured. As soon as the lamp illuminated a bullock, the dog forgot about the rabbit and went berserk tearing into the unfortunate bullock making it bellow with pain and finally 'coming in' on it with such frenzy that it pulled the half-grown bullock off its feet. The noise was cacophanous, the damage done to the bullock almost unbelievable and the upshot of the matter was that my associate, who by the way shouldn't have been on the land anyway, was hurriedly driven away in a police car while a farmer went for a shot gun to put the dog down – an easy matter as the lurcher had latched to another bullock like a bull terrier and was refusing to let go. My associate received a ferocious fine and became extremely bitter with me because, as he said, I had said that the dog was all right. Hence, to this day, I have never again brokered a deal or given my opinion on the merits of a grown dog a friend was considering buying.

But it takes an extremely clever man to ruin a six or eight week old puppy. That is usually left to the buyer, and sadly there are a great many lurchermen who are expert in this department. So obviously the lurcher enthusiast out to seek another lurcher would be well advised to disregard the old hand who advises him to buy a fully grown dog ('you can see what they are going to be shape wise') and settle for a puppy which he can train make or break himself. So the next question is: 'How do I pick a suitable puppy?'

If you've heeded the advice proffered in the preceding pages and decided to go to a professional breeder to buy a definite and genuine cross of one of the three most popular crosses, then advice is about to be given. If you have decided to go for one of these kaleidoscope lurchers composed of more breeds than the Kennel Club has to offer, then I'm afraid you must take pot luck in choosing a puppy – simply pick up the first puppy that ambles toward you and hope for the best. However let us assume that you have decided on a first cross deerhound/greyhound bred by a reputable breeder who has both sire and dam on show. From such a mating, bearing in mind the relative sizes of both sire and dam, the best advice would be to go for a small bitch or dog – not a runt, mind you, with pot belly and staring coat, but a smallish or medium sized puppy preferably with the deep rib cage of the sire and possibly a bit broader headed than the greyhound dam. The bigger puppies can grow to above 30 inches at the shoulder with power to pull down a stag, but with scarcely enough agility to be able to pick up a ferreted rabbit, let alone a lamped rabbit sitting near to a hedgerow. Avoid the thin, spindly type puppy that resembles a greyhound even at this age. Such a puppy may well have speed aplenty but will burn up like a torch and be no more use than a coursing greyhound after a few hard courses. Furthermore, to expect a dog with such a physique to be able to withstand a hard night's lamping would be asking too much of it.

If the buyer's choice is a Bedlington/greyhound hybrid and a breeder of a genuine first cross can be found with a litter bred from a fairly tall Bedlington terrier and a good quality greyhound, then it would be wise not to choose a cloddy type puppy but to go for a moderate-sized animal with a fairly light frame. Bedlington/greyhounds breed fairly true to type and there is little litter wastage brought about by such a breeding. So one could literally take any puppy from such a mating and expect it to turn out a useful medium sized lamping and coursing dog. Frankly very few genuine (that word again) Bedlington greyhound crosses turn out to be the wrong sort; Bakewell of Coalville who bred many such crosses once said that he had bred quite a few which had not turned out to be top class dogs, but he hadn't bred a single puppy which hadn't grown up to at least look the part of the all-round lurcher. Beware however – first cross Bedlington/greyhounds are a fairly homogeneous bunch: the second cross between two Bedlington/greyhound lurchers can produce a litter with an enormous variation varying from 'pure bred' Bedlington terriers to dogs which would pass for track greyhounds, and some very, very odd intermediate dogs indeed.

Good collie/greyhound hybrids are extremely difficult to pick out as puppies. Some will grow into really greyhoundy dogs very close to coursing greyhounds. Others will grow into collie-like curs which would pass for Exmoor collies. Therefore avoid picking the puppy which has a gigantic cranium capable of containing a collie-like brain, for with such a cranium usually goes a collie-like physique. Even a greyhoundy first cross will have stamina to spare – and I mean stamina – and intelligence far above any longdog mix of sight hounds. Perhaps, however the only advice that can be considered as 100 per cent foolproof is to choose a puppy with a long flat back. Such a dog will grow apace and finish up with a reasonably fine greyhoundy shape. However, once again beware the supposed collie/greyhound first cross which aims to be an eye catcher, a show stopper, for a breathtaking beauty has yet to be born from this mating. David Hancock of Sutton Coldfield believes that by breeding from strains of working bearded collies relatively homogeneous results can be produced. So far it seems Hancock could be right, but it would be wiser to wait until Hancock has produced several hundred of these puppies before one passes an opinion on his theory.

The three-quarter-bred collie greyhound may well be a different kettle of fish. In 1983 D. B. Plummer examined the products of seventy-nine litters of three-quarter bred collie greyhounds and found that there was a marked similarity between every male and also a marked similarity between every female. So it would seem that all one had to do was to pick a puppy from such a litter blindfold to produce a top class dog, but far be it for me to question Plummer who has a mania for record keeping (and I must admit he has kindly allowed me access to all his records) but most of the conclusions he came to were based on three-quarter-bred dog and bitch puppies bred from his own stud dog Merle, a curious homozygous dog who just happened to throw nearly identical litters even to a variety of greyhound bitches. I have seen a variety of types, supposedly collie/greyhound to greyhound matings, but unlike Plummer I could not vouch for their authenticity. Hancock has produced some amazingly level puppies by mating a working bearded collie/greyhound to greyhound bitches and these are to the best of my knowledge the only genuine three-quarter-bred rough coated lurchers available. All seemed racy with large intelligent-looking heads, prominent eyes, rough coats and measuring about 25 inches at the shoulder. However once again it has to be said that whereas a collie greyhound/greyhound hybrid which is too heavy to be an all rounder coursing hunting dog is unheard of, some of these hybrids are a little too greyhoundy for my liking – so greyhoundy in fact that several passed musters as track greyhounds at flapping tracks.

51

Concrete advice on actually picking out a healthy suitable puppy is now called for, and to be as brief as possible it should be said that to pick up a puppy which is anything but in first-class health is false economy. My father ran a scrapyard, so as a child I came in contact with a great many itinerant scrap dealers who claimed to be authorities on lurchers. Many advised buying only the runt of the litter as for some reason or other they believed that this was the puppy which would grow into the best adult. Such a sickly puppy might receive more than its share of socialising from the family on account of the fact that everyone seems to take pity on the puppy which is a poor doer, and thus due to this excessive attention the puppy might be a little easier to train. It is however absolute madness to buy an ailing or weakly puppy, and to determine which puppies are in good health, and which are not, is a relatively easy matter.

Puppies with running eyes might have eye irritation due to pine sawdust being used as bedding or ammonia fumes from bedding which has had fresh straw stacked on top of foul. This eye irritation might also be caused by many of the viral infections some of which, such as hepatitis, might well render the puppy dead before it is settled in to its new home. In short, clean bright eyes are a fairly sure indication that the puppy is well and in good health. Don't buy a runny eyed puppy, no matter what the vendor may give as the cause of the complaint.

Pot-bellied puppies with abdomens bulging are also suspect. This is usually a fairly good indication that the puppy needs worming and also a fairly clear sign that the breeder doesn't know his job and is selling an unwormed puppy to a buyer. Most well-reared puppies received their first worming about four or five weeks of age (I worm mine with a piperazine hydrate solution made up by my local chemist when my puppies are three weeks of age) so by the time the puppies are six weeks old they have lost their pot-bellied look. It is easy to worm a puppy, now that safe and easily administered round worm remedies are available, but an unwormed puppy offered for sale is a fairly sure sign of a sloppy, uncaring breeder and should I be offered such a puppy I would immediately set to thinking what other factors (malnutrition, lack of heat) had influenced its rearing.

Tucked-up and dehydrated puppies (just lift the skin on the neck and watch it slip back to normal – if it resumes its shape quickly the puppy is fine, if it doesn't the puppy is dehydrated) are very bad bets and many just don't last the first week after purchase. Even a normal healthy puppy fed on the food the breeder regularly uses to rear litters will scour a little on coming to its new home, simply because of its change of environment. An already dehydrated puppy will therefore

52

suffer quite badly and invariably die if sent to a new home. The causes of dehydration in a puppy can be viral, bacterial or simply the result of a bad chill. The best advice to any potential buyer is don't bother to ascertain what the causes are – just don't buy one. Above all don't handle suspect puppies and then visit another kennel. Remember the most common cause of dehydration in young puppies in recent months is not just a simple tummy upset, but parvo virus, a killer of puppies and adults alike. Many kennels have shut up shop simply because of this infection, so no legitimate lurcher breeder appreciates a time waster who simply flits from kennel to kennel merely to idle away a day looking at dogs – and believe me there are plenty of those in the lurcher world.

D. B. Plummer, in most of his books on working dogs, states that it is bad policy to purchase a puppy the dam of which shows the symptoms of a rather unsightly and totally incurable malady called follicular mange, a type of skin infection which strips the fur from the animal leaving the dog looking very bare and unsightly. Personally, if buying a lurcher from a breeder who was using a greyhound as a dam to breed the lurcher, I should not be too concerned if I found the bitch had lost quite a lot of hair through follicular mange. Many strains of greyhound are plagued by this infection: I actually owned a greyhound bred in the purple and sired by One and Only who looks quite hideous immediately after she has whelped and reared a litter but she soon clears up within weeks of weaning and in six weeks after the last puppy has found a new home she is as bright eyed and bushy-tailed as the day I had her off the track. To date, and I've bred from her four times in as many years, none of the lurchers she has produced have ever displayed any indication of having this unpleasant and messy-looking disease, though I am sure that as soon as the bitches have started to rear their puppies the trouble will flare up again. It's not a serious infection – no-one seems to know a great deal about it, not even top class vets who have specialised in dermatology. But one thing is certain: providing the dog is not subjected to severe stress (I saw a sister of my greyhound develop bad mange after an attack of parvo virus) the complaint does not manifest itself. If a puppy is bought from a greyhound bitch which is obviously suffering from this infection, the puppy may show symptoms of this complaint as it 'teethes', losing its deciduous teeth for permanent ones, but providing the youngster is well fed and also well housed, the problem will be a temporary one lasting only a matter of a week or so. Thus I wouldn't be put off buying a puppy from a reputable breeder simply because the dam of the litter shows signs of follicular mange.

Likewise, I would not turn my nose up at a puppy simply because it had a few fleas. In recent years the flea has become resistant to nearly every form of insecticide. At one time a dusting of Derris (a harmless natural insecticide, still used by 'strictly-organic' gardeners to kill caterpillars) saw off any fleas. These days fleas are not in the least bit bothered by frequent dustings of this powder and in 1983 a race of super fleas seems to have emerged, a flea not in the least bit troubled by some of the most poisonous insecticides known to man. Thus a puppy which has a few fleas is not exactly displaying all the symptoms of neglect one associates with a verminous litter and should the buyer of a rather flea-ridden puppy be prepared to stick at the treatment, using a few different insecticides if necessary, it would need an incredible strain of flea to survive such measures. Do make every effort to get rid of fleas, however. Not only do they drive a dog mad, making him scratch incessantly, but the flea harbours an even more unpleasant parasite, the dog tapeworm and it is impossible to get a dog free of worms if the dog is still host to a family of fleas.

So you've found your breeder, sorted out the type of puppy you want, made sure you've picked a healthy pup, and brought it home. Where do you go from there?

15   *Training*

I was about eight at the time when I met old Bobby Boothroyd, and I don't mean the MP of the same name. The Boothroyd I knew wore cut-away woolly gloves summer and winter alike and resembled old man Steptoe so much that I wondered whether or not the writer of Steptoe and Son had visited the Black Country and seen Boothroyd at some time or other. Bobby stank, and stank so badly that when he came in to trade his pram load of scrap metal into Dad's scrapyard, Dad passed him money at arm's length, and after Bobby had wiped his ever-running nose on the back of his fingerless gloves he walked across to the local, bought a half of bitter and instantly cleared The Snug by sitting next to the fire. No, Bobby wouldn't have been very much at home in Westminster, but of all the ribald crew who used Dad's yard as a trading point, Bobby was the most fascinating, for in spite of the fact that Dad had dealings with gypsies and tinkers galore, it was only Bobby Boothroyd, for all his nasty habits, his smelly front room, with its dust encrusted white china cats, who was a wizard with dogs in general and lurchers in particular. Thus today when I visit a show or so and see badly-trained lurchers kept on tight leashes lest they wander off never to return, I realize that the modern lurcher has not had its full potential exploited. For the scruffy collie bred hybrid lurcher one sees never getting a look in at a show differed little from the dogs which were bred at Boothroyd's home in Burgess Street – except that Boothroyd's dogs were trained to perfection.

It may be a personal preference, but I like to get a lurcher puppy before it is six weeks of age and although a puppy of that age needs a lot more tender loving care than an eight week old youngster there is so much a puppy can learn between six and eight weeks that it's worth the extra effort of rearing such a baby. The time between the sixth and twelfth week of a lurcher puppy's life is the most receptive period of all, and to buy a puppy above the age of three months and to expect to get the best out of it is asking a lot of a dog. As soon as I buy a puppy, I put a collar on it, for a collar is half way to lead training. For an hour or so, puppy will struggle like the devil to get rid of its collar, but after that it will accept the encumbrance and learn to live with it. Many training manuals advise leaving a puppy until it has had all its injections against distemper and similar ills before attempting to train it, for it is madness to take an uninoculated puppy out of doors; but despite what training manuals say, there is a tremendous amount of training which can be done indoors before the puppy is inoculated. One small point, however: for heaven's sake, take only one puppy up for training. It's nearly impossible to train two litter mates to any standard of obedience – I know, for I've tried it.

Get the puppy walking on a lead as soon as possible. Providing one is gentle, patient and persistent the puppy will be trotting around the house on a lead within hours after the lead-training has begun. Lead-training is essential and it is impossible to proceed further without the dog being lead-broken. Disregard fairy tales of poachers and gypsies, whose lurchers have never seen a lead. Perhaps some of these tales may be true, but to train a lurcher to any standard of obedience without first lead-training it is almost an impossibility. Look at it this way. Some of a lurcher's training – most of it in fact – is fun for both dog and trainer. Some of it, however, is odious, and if a dog is not lead-trained it can quite simply bring any part of its training to an end simply by running off. A lead is a guarantee that training can proceed at the pace you require, not just when a dog is in the mood for it.

Start the puppy retrieving as soon as possible. It's amazing how many otherwise good lurchers just simply won't retrieve and just stand over their catch waiting for their owners to come up and pick up the rabbit or hare. It is also amazing the number of stories that are offered as a reason why the dog will not retrieve. Some lurchermen maintain that all they require the dog to do is catch and the owners are prepared to do the rest. What they need is a good coursing Saluki, not a lurcher, because for all their brainlessness and failure to respond to commands, Salukis are superlative hare catching dogs. One lamper I met at Whaddon Chase Show said, 'I put a lamp on a rabbit the dog catches, I put the lamp on another and straightaway it drops the first and catches the second', which, reading between the lines, means 'I just can't get him to bring back to hand!' Yet it is easy to teach a puppy to retrieve and so essential to have a lurcher which brings its catch to hand.

Start young, and six weeks is not too young to begin retrieving training. Get a rabbit skin from anyone who has a working lurcher, or simply pick up a road casualty – there are plenty about – and skin it. Dry the skin by nailing it fur side out to a door and leave it until the skin side of the pelt has dried to a shiny plastic appearance. Roll the pelt tightly and tie it to prevent it unrolling. This is a dummy which will be literally irresistible to any lurcher with a scrap of go about him.

An 8-week-old puppy retrieving an old sock

Forget the use of a rubber ball, forget the rolled up paper. The dummy will be the next best to the real thing and a dog trained to this type of dummy at the age of six or eight weeks seldom if ever fails to pick up rabbits when the lurcher is tried at the real McCoy. The only retrieving pure-bred Saluki I've ever seen was trained on this sort of dummy, and this dog would pick up any rabbit caught and retrieve it to hand. It did, I admit, wander rather aimlessly for a while, rabbit in mouth, but nevertheless it retrieved its catch to hand which is a damned sight more than many lurchers will do. It is seldom that one needs to 'gee up' a puppy to retrieve if one uses a fur dummy, particularly a skin which has a strong smell of rabbit about it. One small point concerning early retrieving lessons: do not get the puppy so wild with excitement that the return to hand degenerates into a tug of war session for the possession of the dummy. I made an awful hash of my first retrieving training session with a lurcher I bought from an *Exchange and Mart* advert, a deerhound/greyhound – or supposedly so, for the puppy turned out to be a rather leggy collie with just a hint of Bedlington terrier about its ears. It trained easily and went wild with excitement every time I took the dummy out of the shoe box I used to keep my lurcher and ferreting equipment in. I too enjoyed the games, particularly the tug of war with the dummy when it retrieved it to hand. Spike grew into a great lamping dog – great from the point of actually catching the rabbits – but he just wouldn't give up his catch to hand until I literally used pressure points on his jaw to release the rabbit. Of course by this time he simply tightened his grip on the unfortunate bunny and by the time he gave up his catch the rabbit was just three pounds of rather bruised ferret meat. My fault entirely. Spike was totally blameless and I eventually gave him away to a relative of mine as a pet. When he was just over ten years old I took him out once again with the lamp as I was staying with relatives near by and wondered if Spike had lost his lamping skills. He bungled three or four catches but finally connected, racing back to hand to give up his rabbit. Well, not quite for I had to practically choke him to make him give up his catch.

Another big 'don't' regarding retrieving training is, 'don't have another dog in the room when retrieving training is in progress'. Your puppy will retrieve or rather pick up readily enough but will resent giving up his dummy if there is the chance another dog will snatch it from him. Having another dog present gives rise to all sorts of problems as I shall explain later – and remember it is easier to prevent faults developing than to correct faults when they have developed.

Above all, don't ever overdo retrieving training, or any training for that matter. About two years ago I watched a youth exercising a dog on a golf course near Redditch and was much taken with the animal, a Norfolk-type dog with a decidedly deerhoundy look about it. The pup was about fifteen weeks old and the youth had purchased the dog from Aubrey Fryer. The dog was obsessed with retrieving and displayed instincts which would have put a springer spaniel to shame. Aubrey would have been proud of the dog and the youth certainly was for he repeatedly threw a ball which the dog dashed after and returned to hand. The boy was an enthusiastic trainer, too enthusiastic in fact, for he threw the ball just a little too often for my liking and I noticed the puppy's waning enthusiasm for the game. Perhaps I should have mentioned the matter to the lad, for I've made numerous mistakes and perhaps I've learned something from them. However, just as it is inadvisable to interfere with the rows and making up of a married couple, it is also unwise to interfere between a youth and his lurcher;

and anyway very few youths consider anyone above the age of thirty knows anything about anything. About a month later I walked the golf course once again and saw the youth with the dog running loose. It had stopped retrieving and now it would have needed an expert, not a youth to rekindle its interest in the game. I've made the same mistakes regarding overtraining and ruined dogs accordingly. My first lurcher was 'sit' mad. I'd conditioned it to sit so often that I had only to stare at the dog to find the poor bewildered devil sitting even when hunting a field.

Perhaps the worst type of lurcher trainer is the nagger, and I've known some of these, men who have invariably started out with labradors and later found an interest in lurchers. A day with them is made miserable for all concerned by the incessant issuing of commands 'Come Tip', 'Stay Tip', 'Up Tip', 'Down Tip', 'Heel Tip', and as I am irritated after a mere hour of this nagging I pity the poor dog who has to perform day in day out. Obedience is one thing but constant nagging is another. After basic obedience training has been accomplished, and the dog is performing reasonably well, a freewheeling relationship between man and dog should begin to form, a relationship which needs the minimum of commands and the maximum of mutual understanding and respect to succeed. Men who buy and sell dogs don't ever get this sort of relationship with a dog, but watch the one dog man, the man who has reared one lurcher and one lurcher alone from a puppy and see the relationship he has with his dog. Take for example Eddie Jones of Wolverhampton, who bought his three-quarter-bred lurcher as a puppy and began work on it as soon as he brought it home. By the time the puppy was six months old it was obedient and willing to please Eddie at any task Eddie set it, and from then the constant and odious training ceased as the two developed a working relationship. To watch Celt work a field for Eddie, or simply put a rabbit out of a bush and course it is a pleasure, with seldom a work spoken and merely a glance or so given between dog and owner. Don't ever overtrain to the point where constant commands tend to mar the development of the dog/man relationship. Many books on gundogs state that dogs kept in kennels train best of all, but while this may be true of gundogs it certainly isn't true of lurchers, particularly collie-bred real lurchers. These need constant companionship to get the best out of them, the sort of 'my dog goes everywhere with me' relationship. A longdog, particularly a Saluki-bred longdog, may not suffer particularly badly from isolation from its owner, for all it is required to do is course and catch its prey; but a real lurcher is the sort of dog owned by the Arighos or the chap featured in *I Walked By Night*, the rustic characters in *It's My Delight*, owners who kept their dogs with them most of the time, the dog living in the house, sleeping at the foot of the bed. Remember that a man is taught as much by the dog as the dog is taught by the man.

'My dog won't come back to me' is a frequent bleat by readers of the popular sporting press, and frankly by the time a relationship between man and lurcher has got to this stage there isn't much one can do to rectify it. The fault is in the early training of the dog, and unless the dog is an absolute lunatic or has a great deal of sighthound blood, the reason for this annoying fault is simply a breakdown in that relationship. It is difficult to cure this fault and far easier to prevent it happening. Develop a relationship with your puppy. Talk to it; don't be afraid to seem a little strange – most lurchermen are strange anyway. Touch its head as you pass it, stroke its ears even when it hasn't done anything to merit praise. If it is kennelled outside, talk to it through the bars of its kennel whenever you pass its kennel. Once the reader has trained a lurcher well and developed an affinity with it he will realise why it is almost impossible to train two lurchers simultaneously, and understand that the men who parade the shows with six or eight lurchers on slips are simply exhibitionists getting some sort of kick out of parading the shows with 'a lot of dogs'. It's a harmless fantasy, this image of being a man who owns a lot of lurchers, but it ensures not one of this man's dogs will ever be properly trained. Above all, do get some relationship between dog and man and some degree of obedience before starting it to quarry. A lurcher has, or should have, a great deal of sighthound blood in its pedigree and sighthounds are bred only to chase. Hence a dog which is not trained properly and not completely obedient becomes an absolute liability when allowed to pursue its quarry. It becomes the nuisance to end all nuisances for it pursues its quarry heedless of all commands and entreaties, mindless of everything except the catch. Even well-trained lurchers get out of control when chasing a rabbit, hare or fox and deer. An unbiddable lurcher becomes a nightmare.

On the subject of unbiddable or uncontrollable lurchers, it's time to talk of training or breaking to sheep. Here, alas, if the lurcher owner fails, he can literally do no more with his dog, as there are few suitable coursing places where sheep are not pastured. Breaking to sheep must be given absolute priority, or the lurcher trainer will never be able to allow his dog off a slip. I admit my heart skips a beat when one of my dogs courses a hare through sheep or a pair of large luminous eyes appears in the beam as I am lamping, but so far, thank God, I've had no trouble with sheep. How to break a dog to sheep is another matter and many books and several authorities recommend taking a puppy amongst sheep while the puppy is very young and tugging its choke lead as soon as it shows an interest in sheep, while the owner mutters a menacing 'No'. Others recommend allowing a puppy to scamper through sheep and when the lurcher shows an interest in the sheep, peppering it with acorns or small potatoes shot from a catapult. This again is a relatively effective method of control, but a puppy struck by a catapult shot tends to panic and hare off through the flock, often causing greater damage to the sheep than it would have done if left unchecked. The good old tried and tested method is of course to take a day trip into the Welsh mountains during lambing time and leave the puppy to the tender mercies of a ewe with newly-born lambs. Don't underestimate the butting power of a sheep. One of my relatives had a knee cap smashed quite badly when an unruly ram decided to defy all efforts to drive it into a trailer. Welsh mountain sheep, both rams and ewes, seem a race apart as far as dogs are concerned, and it is a brave and very stupid puppy that decides to stand its ground when an angry ewe decides she has had enough of the lurcher's attentions. This training to sheep can be overdone, however. One of my own Bedlington/greyhound hybrids is so terrified of sheep that she has to be put on a lead when we approach a flock, not because of the damage of her attacking them, but simply because she panics and tries to run back to the car. When coursing a hare, even when she is hot on a hare, she will 'come off' the course as soon as she runs into sheep. I never get any trouble with her concerning stock worrying but it is a bit of an annoying trait to find in a coursing dog.

While on the subject of sheep worrying, perhaps a mention of the recent mania sweeping the ranks of lurchermen is necessary, and I refer to sheep rustling. About two years ago I was returning home from a lamping session in Leicester when a police car flashed its lights behind me, pulled up in front of me, and asked me to turn out my van. At the time of writing the law regarding searching vehicles in this manner is a bit in favour of the citizen, who can literally refuse to allow a police officer to do this, but I had nothing to hide (and besides I was more than a little frightened) so I opened the van doors and allowed the search. I had six rabbits, two hares and an unfortunate water hen, a road casualty I'd taken home for my ferrets, but the police seemed uninterested in these and didn't even ask if I had permission to lamp in Leicestershire. Furthermore they didn't even check the car over for defects, a regular and irritating occurrence which most night time lampers must learn to accept from the police. They looked at both my dogs, checked their mouths and waved me on, after which they did a Starsky and Hutch turn in the road and raced back to Leicester. I didn't have long to wait to find out why. That night some lunatics with lurchers pulled down, butchered, skinned and gutted some ewes just across the road from where I was lamping and the sight of two lurchery faces appearing in the rear windows of my van made me an obvious suspect for the job. Subsequently I lost my legitimate lamping spot in Leicester, for I was politely asked not to go back there until lambing had ceased and perhaps, the farmer added, it was not such a good idea to run a dog on his land anyway. This taking of sheep is a crazy practice. It is useless to say that sheep stealing is bringing lurcher owners into disrepute for by the very nature of their dogs, lurcher owners have always been in disrepute, but sheep worrying, the mangling of farm animals and the selling of any pieces of carcass still intact after such an onslaught, is certainly turning the general public off the lurchermen. Since time immemorial farmers have turned a blind eye to the village poacher, lurcher at heels, skulking up the hedgerow in pursuit of rabbits, but the sheep thief is another type of creature and no landowner tolerates such a person on his land.

Any lurcher worthy of the name lurcher must be able to jump. At the Lambourn Lurcher Show in 1982, a group of lurchermen were heard to say that they never taught their dogs to jump because lamping dogs allowed to jump in total darkness tend to get themselves killed by jumping into hazards they cannot see. But these same hazards are there for the daytime coursing dog, and, as most lurchers will literally jump any obstacle to get to their hare, the 'don't teach your dog to jump' lamping theory just doesn't hold water. Lurcher-men with non-jumping dogs are lurchermen who simply can't or haven't taught their dogs to jump.

Yet lurchers are incredible jumpers, as anyone who has visited a working lurcher show can verify, and some scale almost impossible heights for the smallest exercise. At the 1979 Game Fair I saw the incredible, much-talked-of, much-disputed jump performed by Plummer's Burke who cleared a mini-bus without touching either the sides or the top. The truth concerning this jump is disputed by many, but Alan Bryant who owned Bryant's Fields Sports, owned the bus the dog actually jumped, and many people photographed the leap. Another famous leap was made by John Granger's collie/greyhound/greyhound hybrid across a twenty-nine foot dyke in Cambridge. This bitch, a rather mousy creature more akin to a whippet than a greyhound, was the most unsuitable type of dog for jumping, yet she cleared formidable obstacles and dykes, and landed without altering her stride. Sadly this bitch came to a sticky end shortly after Whaddon Chase Lurcher Show 1979, when she became dispirited and off-colour and died the same night. Granger always maintained that she died after a particularly strenuous out-of-season course on hare, but the symptoms point to parvo virus, which was rife that year.

So realizing the jumping potential of this type of dog it is difficult to understand why many lurcher trainers just don't teach their dogs to jump. There are few Six Mile Bottom and Salisbury Plain type coursing places in Britain and most other districts which harbour hares are still criss-crossed by hedges through which a hare can slip, but over which a lurcher must jump. The dog which runs up and down the hedge seeking a gap simply doesn't catch hares; and if I had a penny for every man who told me he had a first class coursing dog and then had to lift it over fences, I'd be a rich man indeed.

The teaching of jumping is a piece of cake, providing the lurcher-man is both patient and understanding. The best way I've found, is to start as soon as the puppy is settled in the house and six weeks isn't too young to start simple 'jump training'. Get a piece of board (T&G 4½-inch board is wide enough) and jam it across a doorway. Put the puppy on one side of the board, slip over it and call the puppy to you. It will clamber the board without any difficulty. Do this repeatedly, but again not too often, until it regards the board as a very minor obstacle and hops over it. It is this jumping action that needs to be taught, for many lurchers simply just can't get the notion of lifting their hind legs to jump. Greyhound trainers who train hurdlers tell me they get the same problem starting their dogs. However a puppy which gets into the habit of lifting its hind legs over an obstacle is half way to becoming a good jumper. However don't overdo the jumping training and above all don't let the puppy get upset, frightened or hurt while jumping. Some years ago I took on a lurcher puppy for a friend who said that he just didn't have the time to do it justice (I must add he found the time later when I trained and entered the dog for him). The puppy was the result of a not too careful blend of whippet/greyhound/Bedlington and collie with a bit too much greyhound for my liking. She was six months when he bought her, totally untutored both inside and outside the house, and wet and screamed blue murder when I tried to lead train her, screaming so loudly that one of my neighbours phoned the police and told them I was killing the dog. Within days she was walking on the lead and even showed a moderate interest in retrieving, which is odd, for an untrained six-month-old puppy usually finds retrieving a bit of a puzzle. I started her jumping and while at first she raced up and down refusing to hop across 6-inch T&G board she mastered the knack, and in next to no time she was literally hopping over two feet. Subsequently I made a hurdle for her and encouraged her to leap it, but on her first day she toppled the hurdle and came down with a thump, injuring her hind leg. She never forgot the incident and henceforth refused to jump again. She is now with my friend who lamps her a little and lifts her over fences and gates and can't for the life of him understand why the bitch won't jump hedges, no matter how he coaxes her.

Competitive jumping is quite a big event at lurcher shows, and to compete in any of these jumping events, one needs to train one's dogs somewhat differently. Once again a tiny obstacle is set up in a passage way, but this time a dog on leash is run at the obstacle and the owner steps over, yanking the lead and almost lifting the dog over the jump while giving the command 'Up and over'. Gradually the height of the jump is increased and the dog is required to jump the obstacle as the owner steps over the jump. After a while the boards become so high that the owner of the lurcher must simply run at the obstacle, dog on slip, and shout 'Up and over' as he comes within jumping range of the boards. Against-the-clock obstacle racing at shows is now very popular and some dogs really enjoy it. Collie-bred lurchers excel at this form of activity, as they delight in pleasing their owners. At the time of writing, Alan Hooten, of Doncaster, has one of the most successful obstacle-course hurdlers in the country, but for some strange reason the rosettes gained by winning these difficult contests are never prized as much as the rosettes obtained through winning at a lurcher show which gives prizes for the most attractive animal. Few of the dogs which win regularly in the jumping and hurdling events are ever placed in the show ring. A classic example of this was seen at Durham a few years ago, in a show class of only five lurchers. Four rosettes were given out, and the dog which didn't get a rosette then jumped a set of football goal posts for a bet. Yet not one of the winning four were capable of clearing a jump of three feet.

One small point and then it is time to leave the subject of jumping. Once your dog is jumping well, don't make a fool of him by deliberately jumping him over obstacles which can conceal hazards. More lurchers are killed by landing in ditches, on farm equipment, and on main roads than anyone can imagine. When jumping the dog over barbed wire, spare a thought for its feet and stretch your arm across the top of the wire so that if he touches he comes in contact with your arm not the wire. Wire is hell for running dogs, and, while it may do a fairly good job keeping stock enclosed, the inventor, whom I am told was a woman, could not have foreseen the havoc her ingenious device has caused. This arm-on-the-wire technique is not a foolproof way of ensuring that the lurcher doesn't come to grief, but it helps.

A well-trained lurcher is not only a joy to own but proper training is absolutely essential if one is to use a lurcher as a hunting dog. My spirits plumet whenever I find a fellow lurcher man turn up for a day's coursing or rough hunting with a maniac dog. Some of us do have permission to hunt land, no matter what the sporting press claim to the contrary; but what would the reader, if he were the landowner, say if some lunatic turned up at his place with a lurcher just begging for trouble, cartwheeling on the lead, and so disobedient that contact between dog and human resembled a duel rather than a working relationship. It should now be patently obvious that the reader should at least attempt to obtain some degree of obedience from his lurcher.

16 *Lurcher Shows*

Taplin is quite wrong when he calls the lurcher 'the pariah of the canine world', but one thing is certain, the lurcher owner of pre-1939 days was generally treated as a social outcast: the sort of chap no-one trusted, and furthermore the sort of man no right thinking farmer would employ or willingly invite on his land. D. B. Plummer calls the lurcher 'the hallmark of the disreputable' and he would have been correct to apply this title to the pre-war lurcher owner. To have held a show for lurchers and their owners in those days would have been unthinkable.

Furthermore, the lurcher certainly didn't lend itself to showing. It was, or should be, the all-time greatest illicit hunting dog, and the characters who owned this type of dog were more concerned with its catching ability than its ear carriage, its speed rather than its length of stifle, its toughness and ability to withstand adverse conditions rather than its length of back. All in all, the lurcher fraternity were not particularly show-orientated; and so no country shows involving lurchers and their owners were held – not until 1971, that is.

In 1971, a racehorse trainer called Captain Peter Lowis and his wife, plus a friend of theirs, the artist Leesa Sandys-Lumsdaine, decided to hold a show for lurchers and lurcher types in a paddock at Mr Lowis' home. Sufficient to say Mr Lowis lived at Lambourn and hence the Lambourn Lurcher Show was born.

The first show proved an enormous success (though at the time it had some rather curious publicity from the sporting press) and the £60 profit made from gate entry, sandwich sales etc. was sent to the Injured Jockey's Fund. It was a start, the beginning of the lurcher entering the showdog world, a world which had encompassed (and I hasten to add, invariably ruined) most canine breeds since its beginning in 1859. From such humble beginnings 'it just growed' until in 1981 there were thirty classes and 1,260 entries at the Lambourn Lurcher Show.

Of course the idea of staging a lurcher show caught on, and caught on like wildfire at that. Within five years most hunt supporters groups were staging shows to raise funds for local fox hunts, and gymkhanas soon followed suit. In spite of the fact that, at that time most lurchers

Col. E. G. Walsh judging lurchers at Lambourn 1982

were kept strictly for use, it's a curious type of man who can't find some sort of beauty in the stock he keeps, be it horses, pigs or fish, and lurchers are sometimes extraordinarily beautiful creatures with a flowing grace equal to that of the most elegant show-bred Borzoi. However, with the coming of the shows, came a hitherto unknown respectability for lurcher owners. New types of lurcher owner began to emerge. No longer was the breed the prerogative of poachers and coursers, for, with the advent of the shows, ordinary country folk or folk merely interested in country pursuits, people who wouldn't have contemplated a poaching excursion or a day's coursing and ferreting, began to take an interest in lurchers, and in next to no time the lurcher was vying with that other canine unregistered outcast, the Jack Russell, for the title of the most popular dog breed in the country. Furthermore, a variety of books concerning lurchers began to sprout like mushrooms. Before 1971 only Drabble's rather bitty *Of Pedigree Unknown* concerned itself with lurchers but after the Lambourn 1971 show Simpson's woolly, but readable *Rebecca The Lurcher* appeared, followed fairly rapidly by E. G. Walsh's masterly *Lurchers and Longdogs*, D. B. Plummer's *Rogues and Running Dogs* and later *The Complete Lurcher*; there was also Katherine Tottenham's *All About The Lurcher*, a book designed for those who tend to be a little more respectable than the average lurcher owner. Forty years ago such books would not have found sales enough to justify an adequate print run and mention of them would have brought letters of protest from readers of papers concerned with country matters. Today such books find a ready market, and few sporting periodicals, *Gamekeeper and Countryside* excepted, do not mention lurchers in their columns. The books concerning lurchers, with the exception of D. B. Plummer's books which still cause offence among the more staid of country sportsmen, are now considered respectable reading and the popularity of these books can be appreciated when one considers that the most stolen books from public libraries are books concerning lurchers. Lambourn was responsible for this flush of interest in this breed of dog, and for the rash of lurcher shows which seem to sprout all over the country with the coming of the spring weather.

On the surface of it lurcher shows are such useful affairs that it is a wonder that country people and hunt supporters are rather opposed to this type of sporting event. The show certainly attracts large numbers of people to the district, provides an incredible revenue for stall holders (one ice cream seller claimed to have taken over £1,000 on one of the Lambourn shows), yet there is a sinister side to these shows which is worth considering if one intends to run such an event. But first, the details concerning the typical lurcher show.

Most lurcher shows are summer events, partly because the fine weather is supposedly good for attracting entries and partly because during winter time most members of the lurcher fraternity are reputed to be out coursing, lamping, ferreting and at other lurchering activities. In truth some of the indoor lurcher shows staged at Neath and District and at other working men's clubs in Yorkshire net an incredible sum of money even when staged in the middle of winter. The fact is that many of the folk who frequent lurcher shows do not in all honesty work their dogs all that regularly (if they did there wouldn't be a hare or rabbit left in the country) and these shows at least provide an admirable opportunity for such people to get pleasure from their dogs. The lament of losers, who barrack the judge for his choice of winner, shouting 'That dog has never seen work in its life,' is extremely unjustified. A lurcher show is a show where a judge is allowed to choose which dog he considers to be the best-looking lurcher in the show. It is his opinion, nothing more and nothing less, and in no way reflects the true worth of the dog in the coursing field. Some of the very best coursing and hunting lurchers just don't get a look in at a show. Mick Douglas' Rust was a fairly unsightly brute by any standards, and had faults enough to make the average judge question whether the bitch was a lurcher; yet this bitch was a peerless coursing machine capable of knocking down an incredible number of hares even well into her dotage. The true test of the value of a lurcher is the coursing field, or its all-round hunting ability, and the shows should be regarded as just a bit of fun, and certainly no more than that.

Generally there are several classes for lurchers staged at each show. Some shows even stage a class for collie lurchers, running dogs with a

The rosettes being presented at the Whaddon Chase Show 1983

fair percentage of collie in their make-up; and this class is fascinating because it attracts an amazing rag, tag and bobtail variety of lurchers to its ranks. Dogs which are obviously mongrels with little or no greyhound blood in their make up to dogs which would be quite acceptable at a greyhound flapping track are found in these classes, together with a set of judges who are wishing they were judging somewhere else! These classes are a kind of forlorn attempt to get lurcher breeders to breed away from the more elegant sight hound type lurcher to the more versatile collie bred lurcher; but if this is so, the classes achieve very little, for few collie type lurchers actually win in these classes. The fact is that the wrong sort of judges have set the standards for these shows. Saluki, deerhound, Afghan, and other sight hound breeders are invited to judge at these shows and while it is certain that these people are very competent to judge conformation in any Kennel Club registered breed of sight hound, what is equally certain is the dogs most of these judges pick out as winners are usually far too greyhoundy to be classed as real lurchers.

At one time, only dogs with a high proportion of deerhound blood in their make-up won at these shows and it is easy to see why. Deerhounds have been bred for conformation, long flowing coat and elegant aristocratic looks for generations, so it is not surprising that dogs bred from these beautiful sight hounds were some of the best lookers at the shows. As a result of mating deerhounds to greyhounds or to other lurchers the winners found at the shows in the middle 1970s were whoppers, gigantic elegant beasts scarcely different from a pure-bred deerhound in appearance and real show stoppers. The fact that they were not quite as good on the coursing field, and unable to work as real lurchers was by the way. They certainly attracted a lot of attention, quite a lot of envy and won just about every show staged in the country.

E. G. Walsh was largely responsible for restoring sanity at these shows by his critical articles concerning lurchers and allied running dogs. While Walsh admits that he likes a dash of deerhound in his lurchers he is also aware that some of the very worst dogs seen at shows, 'camels and donkeys' according to Walsh, are bred this way. Walsh made a fairly clear distinction between coursing and working lurchers in his articles, the former being dogs capable of coursing hares and little else, while the latter were dogs more suitable in type size and disposition for the pot-filling task for which these dogs were intended. Furthermore, Walsh set (or rather altered) the standard for these shows by judging lurcher shows and putting up middle-sized dogs, of the type favoured by the poacher and the warrener, rather than the giants which were more at home on the rolling coursing plains than the hedgerow and woodland. Walsh set the pace and others tended to follow suit, until today one seldom finds a 29-inch giant only slightly different from a pure bred deerhound in structure winning at their shows. Today's winners are usually medium sized thick set greyhoundy dogs or Norfolk type lurchers of the type described by East Anglian rabbit catchers of the 1930s. Recently a spate of Bedlington-bred lurchers have dominated these shows. The majority of winning lurchers (large size) are usually between 24–26 inches at the shoulder and more stockily built, built more for hard work than elegance, than the winners of the early lurcher shows of the 1970s.

Just recently, in 1981 to be exact, the National Lurcher Racing Club has set up shows in various parts of the country together with lurcher racing events, obedience tests, obstacle courses and high jumping events. These events are some of the best-organized shows in the country, run by dedicated lurchermen who wish to stage honest-to-goodness dog shows and side events so diverse in their nature that they are bound to please most people. Whether or not the NLRC will do more good than harm to the lurcher is a much debated subject. E. G. Walsh believes that the Sunday lurcher racing events staged by many clubs will at least find entertainment and work for the bored lurcher keeper who might otherwise find himself in court for poaching. D. B. Plummer in his letter to *Shooting News* is not quite as favourable in his evaluation of the club. Plummer considers that the formation of this club could sound the death knell for the working lurcher; for to produce a dog suitable for winning these races (and winning regularly) all one has to do is to dilute the working lurcher blood lines with copious draughts of racing greyhound or racing whippet blood. Plummer (at his gloomiest) sees that in another twenty years this racing lurcher club will produce dogs which may be rough of coat, but genetically they will be little different from racing greyhounds and, while these dogs will perform admirably over the 200–300 yard dashes organized by the club they will be of little use as working lurchers, which should not only have a fair turn of speed, but have instinct enough to work rabbits, hares and feathered game with very little training.

Personally I feel Plummer is being unduly pessimistic, and I for one applaud the excellent work the club is doing. Lurchers have always been catch dogs, dogs of the chase whether they are pushing out rabbits from hedgerows or enduring a grindingly hard course after hares. It seems highly unlikely that any genuine hunter will deliberately water down a really good strain of lurcher merely to breed dogs suitable for these 300 yard dashes (which are staged so rarely,

71

and the prize money so insignificant that only a fool would deliberately breed a dog only for such events). It may also be of interest to add that Lambourn saw many lurchers race against track greyhounds over a straight but short course chasing after dummy, and it was seldom that a greyhound finished up as the ultimate champion of the racing. The people attending the NLRC are seldom interested in simply winning a series of races, and usually attend such meets simply to enjoy the social event. The fools who do set out to breed a lurcher suitable only for racing in these heats would find the whole business very unprofitable and in next to no time would be back to racing pure-bred greyhounds on the flapping tracks. Long may the NLRC flourish! The Club organizes the best lurcher shows and gives the maximum entertainment for the entrance fee.

During the last few years some shows have staged obedience tests as well as racing and dog shows at their lurcher/terrier hunt supporters shows and these are well worth attending. Very few lurcher men consider competing in such events; not because such contests are not considered worth while, but quite simply few lurcher men seem capable of winning events which require the dog to be trained to any standard of obedience. This event, far more than the shows or lurcher racing sorts out human sheep from human goats. Dog dealers with ten dogs on slips, each dog for sale, don't get a look in on these events which require a good relationship between dog and man, a relation-ship brought about by constant and loving contact. The reader would do well to disregard the supercilious attitude of the man who offers ten dogs for sale and avoids the obedience tests supposedly 'on principle' and realize that such an attitude is brought about by the sour grapes syndrome. Few dogs without a good proportion of collie blood succeed in their obedience tests, and seldom if ever is the omni-present deerhound/greyhound or saluki/greyhound entered for this com-petition. Some lurchers can be trained to an amazing standard of obedience even while other dogs only a stall away are chasing a dummy hare. Alan Hooten of Doncaster and Vermeuil of Stratford are two very successful competitors in obedience tests and both use three-quarter-bred collie/greyhounds, the standard of obedience of which has to be seen to be believed.

The jumping contests are also excellent ways of separating the men from the boys (or rather the truthful from the fabricators) and before explaining the last statement it might be best to state that it is nearly impossible to catch hares during a daytime course with a dog which is reluctant to jump. Hares use hedges like a postman uses shortcuts and run up and down dry stone walls like spiders. Thus a dog which cannot jump will come unstuck against such hares, and a tale will explain my original statement. Some three years ago I visited a South Wales lurcher show and listened to a man who rambled on about the hare-killing prowess of his dog. No hare it seems, was safe from this wonderful dog which had only to see a hare to be on it in a trice and retrieving it to hand. This dog had never missed a hare, the owner lied, but his tales came to an abrupt halt when he entered his dog for the hurdle race, a race which involved the dogs hopping over a series of rather low wicker hurdles, which certainly wouldn't have taxed the jumping skills of a second rate greyhound. He slipped the dog after the dummy hare and the lurcher raced to the first hurdle and then simply ran up and down not knowing how to jump the wicker fence. The braggart's credibility died at this point; and if I remember correctly, he returned silently to his car, dog on slip and left the show. Some lurchers develop a knack of scrambling over the obstacles which get progressively higher as the competition goes on, and more and more dogs either fail to get over the jump, or more often than not jib the jumps completely. The more successful dogs usually learn to hit the jumping boards about halfway to the top of the jumping and slither and roll the rest. Exhibitors competing in these events should be certain that the jump hurdle is properly constructed because, for all their hardiness and toughness, lurchers are sensitive creatures and a jump obstacle falling on top of the dog usually ensures that the lurcher will refuse any further competitive jumping. Three-quarter-bred collie/greyhounds or at least lurchers with a fair proportion of collie blood usually monopolize these events, for collies not only seem to live to please their owners, but many are remarkably good at scaling outsized jumps.

Jumping against the clock, urging a dog over a set of five-bar gates is great fun particularly as after a while the more cute of lurchers simply jump one or two obstacles and then run alongside the gates to the finish. Often such a contest is a test of the owner's speed as much as the lurcher's, for the man must run alongside the dog.

These events are invariably treated as jokes by the showdog owner, but they are a far better indication of the dog's athletic prowess than walking him up and down in front of a judge.

So a lurcher show can well be a first class Sunday's entertainment for all the family at a cost of only a fraction of the price of a visit to a cinema; and some five years ago this was absolutely correct. These days things aren't quite as pleasant. A rather nasty element started attending the lurcher shows, the sort that are more at home at a Broadmoor Old Boys reunion than a country sports fair and this element too 'just growed' as the shows became more popular. Various groups of gypsies and tinkers started to come to Lambourn and similar shows – not the gypsies described in Manfri Wood's book or in Smith's *The Silent People*, but the worst of the itinerant families out not to watch a show but hell bent on spoiling one. Youths, given Dutch courage by trips to the beertent, began to annoy exhibitors; and bad losers started venting their spleen on winners and judges alike. At one or two shows reports of lurchers being poisoned came to the notice of the press who gave the incidents just a little too much publicity, but after a while things began to get much worse.

At Lambourn, 1980, a pair of tinker boys settled their arguments both publicly and bloodily and the battle of these two drunken idiots attracted more notice than the Champion of Champion ring. Later a rather nasty incident occurred as the same band of idiots were leaving the show. Next year the Hampshire Long Dogs show promised to be an excellent event, but it was ruined by a very nasty battle which involved a car being turned over and a child frightened very badly. I vowed not to visit the show again, but I needn't have bothered. The organizers got together, discussed the whole messy sordid business, decided the police would be powerless to stop such madness and promptly cancelled the show – a great tragedy as this was one of the highlights of the lurcherman's calender. Other shows experienced the same problems and after the various committees had met to discuss their difficulties they too decided to cease holding lurcher shows. Several members of the Master of Foxhounds Association promptly stopped hunt followers staging lurcher shows to raise money for the hunts. It just didn't seem worth while – the damage done by louts often far exceeded the funds raised by the show. Furthermore the normal lurcher enthusiasts (those interested in lurchers rather than drunken brawls) stopped attending the shows. E. G. Walsh, in his inimitable manner, wrote a calm and sensible article for *Shooting Times* appealing for the louts to stop spoiling the shows and predicting that other clubs would simply stop holding these shows if the rowdy behaviour didn't stop, but once again there was worse to come.

Lambourn is, or rather was, a spectacular show. Held in one of the best venues imaginable on the first Sunday in September it was a date not to be missed, and the weather was invariably fine. In fact it would be difficult to find a more pleasurable day out. The organization of the show was first rate, there were no snags and problems regarding the running of the three rings and everything usually went as smoothly as clockwork. To find an unpleasant incident occurring at Lambourn was once as uncommon as finding a drunken brawl occurring at Lourdes. However 1982 marked the end of Lambourn, and sadly I was there to witness the cause of the cessation of the show. Lambourn has always been a rich kaleidoscope of people, with, as Walsh puts it,

Romany dicklos as common as regimental ties; but once again the lunatic fringe became rather too numerous.

It was such a popular show that many exhibitors came a few days before the show and 'camped out' in readiness. 1982 saw a particularly unpleasant band of campers, a crowd which would have put paid to a Butlin's holiday camp let alone a sleepy Berkshire village. The year in question, story has it, assaults both physical and sexual occurred in the village and the inhabitants of Lambourn were well and truly fed up before the show began. Bands of idiots ran riot on the downs running hares when available and coursing sheep when hares were in short supply and by the Sunday morning the villagers and farmers had had more than enough of the once well received Lambourn Lurcher Show. The national press had probably been alerted to expect trouble and sent several reporters to the show, some of whom gave remarkably truthful accounts of the show, while others must have attended a totally dissimilar function if their accounts were anything to go by.

Just before the judging finished, the crowd suddenly left the show-ring to watch a bare knuckle battle between two Romanies who, battered and bleeding, set about each other like wild beasts. Several cameras were broken by supporters of both contestants but one or two good photographs were taken and these were bought by reporters. Bare knuckle battles are common where Romany families are concerned and they are often colourful and dignified affairs, the only way of settling tribal differences that Romany people seem to understand. They are invariably very private affairs reserved for tribal meetings at horse fairs such as Appleby where the battles are conducted, matters of honour settled and both tribes daub their faces with the blood of both fighters. This battle however was in front of the general public, a messy, unsightly brawl without dignity or tribal tradition. Of course the newspapers went wild with delight and wrote up a weekday spectacular on the whole show, fabricating quite a lot of the detail, and adding an account of a cock fight and a badger bait that seemingly went hand in hand with the battle. Overnight the sleepy, rather exclusive village of Lambourn developed an image which resembled Hogarth's Gin Street. I attended the show and while it must be admitted that the bare knuckle battle did take place, the story of the badger bait and the cock fight were ludicrous. Game cocks have always been sold at country fairs, but the selling of game cocks is one thing, the fighting of them is a different ball game. This bare knuckle battle, the dreadful publicity, the pre-show idiocy, the madness of the bands of supposed field sport supporters, tipped the scales as far as the Lambourn Lurcher Show committee were concerned. Hence I find the first Sunday in September completely free and sorely miss Lambourn. Whaddon Chase or Chatsworth or even Lowther may now become the principal venue of lurchermen, but how long will it be before these shows too are wrecked by rowdies? Lurchermen – you are cutting your own throats! Always leave 'em laughing is the old music hall adage. At Lowther 1983 the committee decided that if there was any trouble the lurcher show would be cancelled for ever after. E. G. Walsh was asked to address the assembled lurchermen before the show and such was the impact of his speech that the spot of trouble which did occur was quickly quashed by genuine lurchermen.

17 *Lamping*

This is my kind of sport, the pursuit of rabbits or hares with a lurcher, the prey illuminated with a beam of light. There are few sports to equal it, there is no sport to better it.

A hundred years ago, the most productive method of rabbiting was long netting, a process which involved the driving of rabbits by night into a long net stretched between the feeding ground and the warrens. Jefferies and other authorities mention that sometimes during a boom in the rabbit population, hundreds of rabbits could be taken during a night's long netting. Big hauls certainly were made, but while a night's long netting could be highly remunerative (particularly with rabbits fetching 25p a piece, as they did during the meat rationing period during and after World War II) the exercise could be dreary, tedious, lengthy and seldom if ever exciting. The long net was also the principal piece of equipment for the pre-war poacher; but the risks a long-netting poacher took often far outweighed the profits he expected from his night's illegal long-netting. Whereas it is easy to whistle in one's lurcher and depart under cover of darkness, a long net takes a considerable time to set and an equal period of time to dismantle. In fact so many long nets were confiscated by police between the wars that they were auctioned off once a year in some districts; and at these auctions the landowners frequently bid against the poacher to gain possession of these nets, to ensure that these handmade nets were destroyed rather than used again to catch quantities of game and rabbits.

These days, when myxomatosis has made such inroads into the rabbit population it seems almost incredible that the recorded pre-war rabbit populations could exist in this country and there are few places where long-netting will be justified by the haul of rabbits one could expect. The coming of myxomatosis in 1953 marked the beginnings of grim times for warreners. Most went out of business after 1955 and the ferret became almost a novelty for years after that time. Long nets were simply not practical with such a scarcity of rabbits, and, with the passing of the coney, the users and makers of these nets began to forget their skills, until today even though the rabbit population looks like reviving due to an immunity to myxomatosis there are precious few men who can claim to be truly proficient at the art of setting a long net.

However as one door closes another opens, and man, being an inventive creature by nature, began to devise other methods of taking rabbits. During pre-war days the landowner could enjoy an evening's rabbiting by driving around the fields in an old car at night, with a friend seated on the bonnet or strapped to the roof shooting the rabbits which appeared in the beam. Equally inventive rabbit hunters were wont to slip a dog, usually a whippet, from the moving car while endeavouring to keep the rabbit in the beam while the whippet ran the rabbit down. Whippets are preferable for the act of being slipped from a moving car at rabbits, as they are usually far superior to a lurcher in take-off speed and they have an inbred gift of being able to come down in stride after being thrown, for whippets were raced to a rag, not from traps like a greyhound, but by being flung towards the rag by a 'slipper'. Old warreners and equally old coursing men can usually tell fascinating tales of hunting rabbits by night with a whippet slipped from a car and if these tales are true then the whippet of those days must have rivalled the lurcher as the all-round hunting dog, though tales of over a hundred rabbits taken by a whippet slipped from a moving car should be treated with just a hint of suspicion! Still a trip to Dudley or Brierly Hill is a must for any collector of tales concerning the very sporting whippet.

The car batteries of those days were tremendously heavy, equal to that of a modern lorry, and a man would have been hard pressed to carry such a battery across a flat field let alone over ditches, walls and hedges. This would have made an evening's lamping a tedious back-breaking hell rather than a pleasure. However during the 1950s considerable research went into producing a light, easily transported battery which would still hold a considerable charge of electricity. Research is still going on to produce even lighter and more efficient batteries which, one day in the not too distant future, will drive electrically powered cars. These days, light batteries are cheap and readily available, and this coupled with the fact that there are now an incredibly large variety of beams available, beams varying from pencil thin affairs to lamps which will illuminate an area nearly a mile away, have made lamping the principal method used by professional rabbit catchers and poachers these days.

Firstly, before the lamper considers buying and training a lamping lurcher, or purchasing or building a lamp, the potential lamper should realize one thing. The public consider that lamping is unsporting as they believe that once a rabbit or hare has a lamp switched on it, it freezes into immobility and is easy meat for any dog to catch. This just

78

A lurcher about to pick up its rabbit

isn't true. Catching rabbits on a lamp requires a skilful lurcher, adept at picking up a moving rabbit or hare. Rabbits move just as quickly and are just as nimble during the hours of darkness as by day.

Why therefore is lamping a more productive method of rabbiting than simply taking the dog out during daylight hours and hunting up rabbits? Well the answer is that rabbits are not strictly diurnal, which means feeding by day and most decide to venture abroad by night to feed, and as Locksley says, to play, for play takes up a great deal of the private life of the rabbit. Rabbits will rarely travel far from the burrows during daylight hours and simply sit outside their warrens cleaning themselves and eating their own faecal pellets, a disgusting but essential habit which ensures that the rabbits' intestines get every chance to digest the rough grass on which most rabbits feed. At night time rabbits stray a great distance from the warren to graze. One

Bromsgrove allotment holder once phoned me to stop the rabbit damage on his allotment and was so exasperated with the mess the rabbits had made of his cauliflowers, carrots, cabbage and particularly runner beans that he offered to pay me a pound a head for every rabbit caught. I went to his allotment and looked for a rabbit warren, but try as I might I couldn't find one. Garden sheds, under which many rabbits choose to live yielded nothing, but rabbit damage was evident: nibbled shoots, pellets and scuffs, patches of ground dug by rabbits simply to keep their hands (paws) in, were everywhere. Frankly, I was just a bit at a loss for what to do, and allotment holders who are not usually well acquainted with the crafts involved in hunting are a bit impatient and usually expect instant results. I was about to pack up, declare that I was beaten and accept the sneers of the cabbage grower when one of my border terriers began wandering off along some playing fields which adjoined the allotment. About eight hundred yards away he began to dig at a hole and barked frantically at whatever was inside. I let the place settle for an hour or two, put in a ferret and netted four rabbits. Damage to the allotment ceased forthwith.

Another tale will perhaps illustrate the point a little more unpleasantly. One of Birmingham's characters is a chap of about thirty-five, heavily tattooed, extremely smelly and excellent company when not in his cups. Sadly, he is frequently drunk and when so charged with liquor he literally runs amok. I came to know him well when one of my dogs sired a litter of puppies to a lightly built lurcher of pedigree unknown, but with quite a lot of whippet in her ancestry. The puppies were of dubious worth and I was about to pass up my choice of litter in lieu of stud fee when my smelly friend turned up at the house offering to buy one of my adult lurchers. I'm a bit touchy about people trying to buy a trained lurcher, as a refusal often means the dog is stolen about a week later, so I offered him the puppy for a pound to get rid of him. Actually, he never paid me the pound, but this has little to do with the tale, so it is wise to pass on. The puppy grew into a rather hideous dog, roach-backed from its Bedlington ancestry, slape coated and rather malevolent to look at. However between Smelly's stints in Winson Green Prison it became a reasonably good lamper. One day Smelly lamped the land near a motorway and found the rabbits were scurrying across the motorway to feed on the second crop of clover and grass that pops up after the corn is cut. Smelly is not very bright and the end of the tale is a little obvious.

So to summarize, lamping is productive not because the rabbits are easier to run by night – they aren't – but simply because the bunnies are prepared to feed away from home after dark and this gives the lurcher a sporting chance.

Of course lurchers are not the only dogs which will perform well chasing rabbits down a beam of light, and any seasoned lamper will have a whole load of tales to tell about amazingly good whippets, collies and even Alsatians whose owners have suddenly decided on a few hours' sport, hunting rabbits at the local cricket pitch and have found their dogs have adapted well to the sport in an amazingly short time. However, before we discuss the most suitable dogs for the job, it would be a good idea to evaluate the qualities a dog must have to make it a good lamper.

Rabbits may feed up to half a mile from home, but the majority of rabbits caught by lampers are the result of a short sharp dash of maybe fifty to a hundred yards. Very large dogs, dogs with a large percentage of deerhound in their ancestry, are usually very fast once they have time to pick up speed and can easily come up on a hare, but such dogs are not particularly useful when they are slipped at a rabbit which is only fifty or so yards from home. What is needed is a nippy dog with the responses of a whippet, and a fair, but not a really great turn of speed. Thirty inch giants look the part, but they don't really get a look in when lamping rabbits. Furthermore the large dog is at yet another disadvantage. Most lamping dogs run into trouble with gates, posts, trees and (alack and alas) wire, at some time in their lives, and many are a mass of scars as a result of their collisions. Furthermore the number of lamping dogs which come to grief through running into these obstacles is staggering, which is probably why dealers make such an excellent living out of selling trained or partially trained lamping lurchers. Large dogs weighing upwards of sixty or so pounds are usually very badly injured when they collide at full speed with a tree stump or fencing post. Lightly built whippety dogs involved in the same type of collision running at roughly the same speed are often winded, sometimes badly bruised, but recover well enough to run another day. On the subject of collisions and the ever popular deerhound/greyhound cross I have a tale worth telling. I wrote a rather derogatory article on the deerhound/greyhound hybrid for *Shooting News* and received a salvo of abuse from a gentleman in Liverpool who not only bred 100 per cent real McCoy deerhound/greyhounds using a cast track greyhound bitch and a rather heavily built Ardkinglas bred deerhound dog, but actually lamped two of the progeny, two steel-grey brindle rough-coated 29-inch dogs. My critic wrote me a stinging letter, phoned me repeatedly and then requested that I came up to Liverpool to see how wrong my article was, for only dogs of this breeding were of any use on the big fields around

Liverpool! Against the advice of friends and family, I went up to see the giants run and found the owner an obliging enough man with a well-trained brace of very elegant deerhoundy lurchers. That night I saw few catches to make me change my opinion about this type of lurcher's ability as a lamp dog, but I saw the most sickening collision of dog and post I have ever witnessed, a collision which not only shattered most of the dog's bones, but fortunately killed the lurcher outright. I returned home and treated my own rather frail and scruffy pair of lurchers with a new respect.

It is also asking a lot of one of these giants to pick up a bobbing, weaving rabbit by lamplight, a rabbit that is making the best use of shrubs, bushes, brambles and hollows as it makes its way back to the warren; and it requires a very agile dog to snap up rabbits as they try to flash through a hedge to safety. Just occasionally one of the big guys gets to learn the knack of doing this: an example which comes to mind is David Hancock's Timmy, a very bold, game, pied, bred from a track greyhound and a half bred collie greyhound. Timmy will literally throw himself at a seemingly impossible angle to catch sneakers which are trying to get through a hedge, but the majority of dogs of this size are simply not up to the task of lamping in small fields and good as some large dogs are, medium to smallish lurchers are usually better.

One criticism of the whippety lurcher, of the rather frail type of dog which has a rather slender frame is that this crossbred lacks stamina and there is perhaps just a hint of truth in this criticism. Many finely built dogs have a tremendous turn of speed, but a slow recovery rate after a hard and taxing run, and these dogs tend to burn out after a hard night's lamping. True, most stockily built dogs are able to call on incredible stamina right up to the end of the night's lamping. Certainly the most outstanding dog that comes to mind when one talks of stamina was the result of mating a large coursing greyhound bitch of pedigree unknown to a big powerful black and gold Alsatian. Frank Delaney, a traveller whose family traded with my father, swore by this cross and there has probably been no dog to top this hybrid for stamina. As with most of these crosses it resembled a lightly built Alsatian with tucked up loins, spare lean shape and murderous disposition. I have certainly seen better catch dogs, dogs for picking up rabbits, indeed I have owned better, but long after my own dogs were spent and blown this ugly mongrel continued to run. Perhaps D. B. Plummer (*Shooting Times*, 1981) is correct when he refers to the Biblical quote 'fat of the mighty', for heavily built lurchers are usually able to run for longer periods than more lightly built dogs. Of course Salukis and some Saluki/greyhound hybrids are the exception to the rule for to give this breed and its long dog crosses its due, they certainly have stamina aplenty.

Nose is unimportant in a lamping dog; indeed it is a disadvantage, for if a dog is adept at hunting up quarry, as soon as the dog loses its rabbit or hare at night, it tends to put its nose down and hunt by scent. Thus many lurchermen refuse to run a dog by day lest it picks up the habit of hunting by scent. It is impossible to break a lamping dog of this habit of hunting up once it becomes set in its ways. Plummer in *The Complete Lurcher* suggests that hunting up can be remedied by running the dog from a slip, and while this method does allow the lamper to walk up the dog until it has view of the quarry (most 'hunters' are too preoccupied with the scent of the quarry to look down the beam unless held, head high, on a slip) it does not remedy the chaos which follows, once the rabbit (or worse still, the hare) goes out of beam and the dog commences to hunt up.

Perhaps the worst night lamping I've ever had was with a Telford based lurcher man I once met at Whaddon Chase. He mentioned he had permission – a lie as it turned out – to lamp an estate fully stocked with pheasants near Bridgnorth and he invited me over for the night. His dog was a useful-looking beast of Norfolk type, the sire of which (he assured me) was featured in E. G. Walsh's *Lurchers and Longdogs*. We arrived at the estate and flashed the lamp around the field, and the rabbit population was literally staggering. He slipped his dog on a rabbit I considered too difficult and the dog not only failed to catch but ran head down on the plentiful rabbit scent driving everything to ground heedless of the silent whistle, the slapping of thighs to attract the dog's attention, and finally the shouts and curses of my companion. Eventually we caught up with the dog but had to run from an angry farmer who ploughed after us in his Land Rover.

Retrieving is one big must for the lamping dog, and a dog which fails to retrieve no matter how good a catch dog it becomes is not really all that useful as a lamper. I've often wondered if the reason why most owners of Saluki/greyhound hybrids look so fit is because they get as much exercise as the dogs picking up the rabbits and hares, for this cross is notoriously bad at retrieving – particularly if required to retrieve the rabbit to the lamper while the lamper has another dog on a slip. While it must be admitted that these dogs are superlative coursers of hares they are not really the ideal dog for the lamper, though I must confess I've seen one or two supposedly genuine Saluki/greyhounds that were top rate on the lamp. The majority of these crosses wouldn't find kennel room with a regular lamper, however.

Unless the dog has a fair percentage of collie or non-sight hound blood, retrieving is apt to become more and more of a chore as time goes on. Some long dogs seem willing to retrieve while still fresh, strong and unwinded, but as the evening goes on the lamper usually finds that these dogs are keen to stand over their prey like coursing greyhounds rather than retrieve it to hand like a lurcher. Longdogs need long and intensive training at retrieving dummies and dead rabbits if they are to be of any use as lampers, and the training needs to proceed at a fairly exciting pace, for such hybrids lose interest very quickly. Furthermore if a true lurcher stops retrieving, jibs, or quits, a week's interesting refresher course will usually put it right again. Once a longdog jibs, there is precious little a lurcherman can do about it, except to get himself very fit to run up and pick up the rabbits his dog has killed. It is frustrating to give refresher courses in retrieving to a useful and otherwise very reliable lamping dog but once a dog switches off its interest in retrieving, it's the only way to ensure the dog doesn't flatly refuse to retrieve forever after.

So having discussed what qualities a top grade lamping dog needs in order to earn its keep, perhaps it is time to suggest which types of lurcher are the most suitable for the job in hand. One of the more popular first crosses is the Bedlington/greyhound hybrid, a first cross which seldom exceeds 23 inches at the shoulder and usually has a first class weather-resistant coat. Forget the fact that most of these first crosses have a decidedly dopey look about them; it's a look they invariably lose as soon as they are taken lamping. Shape wise, they seem ideal for the job in hand and it is small wonder the cross has such a following. Don Bakewell of Coalville who bred such a cross, sold most of them to lampers, and had few dissatisfied customers. Most of these hybrids are very wiry and agile and come off a collision with a fence or wire extremely well as a result of these qualities. D. B. Plummer in *Rogues and Running Dogs* suggests that the cross has a tendency to be hard mouthed, but personally I believe hard mouth is a fault developed during training or misuse rather than an inbred quality, and I know of few Bedlington/greyhound hybrids who are naturally hard mouthed.

Another criticism levied at this cross is that they are prone to be a little too keen on sheep (due no doubt to their terrier ancestry) to be safe as lamping dogs. Again, there seems to be little to substantiate this criticism. Collie lurchers can be equally bad, if not ten times worse, at sheep worrying if left to run riot and most lurchers need to be kept under control at all times anyway. If one weighs up the pros and cons, the Bedlington/greyhound bred from the right type of working Bedlington with keen hunting instinct and bags of fire mated to a good class coursing greyhound must be one of the two obvious choices for a lamping lurcher.

The other choice is the collie/greyhound. This cross is also very popular among lurchermen who lamp rather than course for the first cross collie greyhound is usually a little too stocky for coursing. However, nearly every collie greyhound in a litter of puppies will be fast enough for lamping and game enough for a long tiring night of work as well. The typical cross bred certainly doesn't look much and most look decidedly mongrelly but few breeders and users of this first cross have anything but praise for this very durable type of dog. David Hancock of Sutton Coldfield has this to say of the first cross collie greyhound lurcher:

> I breed only three-quarter bred collie greyhound crosses and first cross collie/greyhound hybrids. As all round hunting dogs, the three-quarter bred has the edge, as it is fast, has a good level of stamina and is a good general all round coursing and working lurcher. However, as a lampdog, a dog required to put in a hard, daunting, cold night's work under quite bad conditions and over rough and woody land, the half-bred collie/greyhound is unbeatable. The stamina of these dogs has to be seen to be believed. Many will run rabbit after rabbit over long arduous courses without so much as panting let alone quitting, and I can honestly say that I have yet to see one of these first crosses tested to the point of exhaustion. From time to time I breed other crosses to order but for my own choice there is only one breed of lurcher for lamping and that is the first cross collie greyhound, bred for preference from a leggy collie from a strain of working border or working bearded collie and a good class coursing or very large track greyhound. Small, undersized greyhound bitches are not really suitable for mating to collies as they have neither frame nor substance to level out the collie shape in the puppies. It is proof enough that customers who order first cross collie greyhound dogs come back here for replacements and if one lamper buys a puppy from this cross within a year nearly all his friends buy puppies from me. Lampers who want a dog to work and as a companion rather than to look at, use this type of dog.

Praise indeed, but there are some who are not quite as enthusiastic about this cross. Aubrey Fryer who has also experimented with this cross says that he has seldom seen a first cross with speed enough to suit him.

In October 1983 *Shooting News* published an article of mine concerning the merits and failings of the collie/greyhound lurcher, and subsequently I received a letter from a Mr Silcock who lives near Stevenage. Silcock bought a puppy from a friend who mated a good class track greyhound to a border type collie from a watcher from Romney Marsh (shepherds in this marsh are called 'watchers' by the inhabitants of the marsh). Silcock states that he was allowed second choice from the litter, the first choice being claimed by the owner of the bitch. Silcock was a little less than happy about the early days of the puppy, for while he admits the puppy trained easily it was the very devil to start and refused to pick up until it was fifteen months old though it would course rabbits well enough and even bowl them over. Once the puppy learned to catch, it worked very well but it was well behind a mongrel bred lurcher of the same age until it was seventeen or eighteen months old. From that age on it became a 'wonder dog'.

D. B. Plummer can also claim to be an authority on this first cross collie greyhound lurcher. He says of it

> This is perhaps the most versatile of the lurcher types, but as a lamping dog it is scarcely the lurcher for the first dog amateur. Many are ultra-willing to please, very easy to train with kindness, but also easily ruined by harsh treatment. When entered carefully and meticulously there seems to be nothing this type of lurcher will not do but it suffers irreparable damage from misuse. If this type of dog has a fault then it is that in its early days it endeavours to catch a rabbit with its feet. Some of these first cross lurchers are fast enough for hare, all will catch them with ease on a lamp as the cross has an unique gift regarding being able to predict movement and turning of the hare. Such is the intelligence of this hybrid that if the lurcherman is a one dog man he will develop a strange relationship with the crossbred and learn as much from the lurcher as the lurcher does from the man. This cross-bred is easily ruined by frequent changes of ownership and any lamper wishing to work such a dog must not sell the lurcher at the first failure, but persist until the dog masters the techniques of lamping.

Lamping is not everyone's cup of tea, not by a long chalk. It is often cold, the results are scarcely predictable, and the haul dependent largely on the darkness of the night and the force of the wind. Many people try the sport, realise the hardships involved and promptly quit and go back to watching television. Thus the newcomer to lamping would be wise not to spend too much on his initial lamping kit and build his own lamping outfit rather than spend a fortune on buying an expensive ready-made lamping kit. A visit to a scrapyard and a spot of ingenuity, and the lamper can acquire serviceable equipment literally for a song. A motorcycle battery in good workable condition takes a little shopping around to get, but a spotlight is easily obtainable and for very little at that. To connect the spotlight to the battery and attach a switch of sorts to the spotlight, binding and insulating it with tape is child's play, and thus a lamping kit has been constructed for a very small amount. I made my first lamp this way and I still have the equipment today. It is essential, however, to have a good serviceable rucksack – nothing special but durable and tough – and it is wise to enclose one's lamp in a plastic container; a cut down gallon detergent or vinegar bottle is ideal. Pad this with paper or foam to prevent the battery rattling around in the container and getting damaged or broken. The plastic container is essential. Batteries subjected to the bumping and banging one gives them during a night's hard lamping tend to leak and the acid plays havoc with the rucksack and one's clothes. My first lamping kit was carried in a cutaway lady's handbag I found in the boot of an old car – a carrier which causes nudges and funny looks when I walk out in public. However the looks stopped after a month or so when the handbag fell apart because the acid ate into it. My jeans also went the same way, and I really had some very odd looks when I walked into an all night cafe for a sandwich after a night's lamping. At that time I stood in greater danger of being prosecuted for indecency than poaching! A kit so built can cost, at the time of writing, as little as £3 and still be very serviceable. If broken or damaged, the parts can easily be replaced by a visit to another scrap yard. The kit won't look very professional, but it's curious that most of the regular lampers, the chaps who have been doing it for years, don't carry fancy kits, but have the same functional Heath Robinson devices I've just described.

After a night's lamping it is wise to check one's kit before going to bed. Batteries will invariably need topping up with distilled water and the battery should be examined for cracks and leaks. A wipe over for the spotlight is a good idea, for it's surprising how much muck and grime adheres to the glass during a night's lamping, particularly if the lamping has been conducted during a wet spell when mud is splashed up at every step one takes. Connections need checking daily, for it's annoying to find one's lamp going off at a critical moment in the hunt – and it's at critical moments that lamps seem to go wrong.

Soldiers going into battle regularly check their guns as a matter of course. A lamper should give his lamp and battery the same respect and a battery treated properly will last almost indefinitely.

Many lampers paint in the beam with black paint, until only a small spotlight of light is visible. This, they argue, narrows down the beam of light and prevents the light striking up which they claim makes the lamper visible from a great distance. Police officer friends of mine – officers who have arrested numerous lampers – tell me that this painting in a spotlight is bunkum. A thin fine light playing around a field is very suspicious and worthy of close investigation, whereas a broad beam playing on a field might on first sight be taken for a motorbike about to be parked. A fine beam of light (and some paint in the beam until only a fine spotlight is visible) certainly doesn't help the dog and such a beam cannot illuminate the dips and hollows of the adjacent land, hazards into which a dog might well run and come to grief. It's a matter of taste I suppose, and the majority of the poachers I've met enjoy having a little mystique about their craft and equipment – and, I hasten to add that most lampers are inclined to poach from time to time.

A recent innovation, and one I'm not all that certain about, nor am I convinced it works, is the use of the red filter, a glass filter fitted to the front of the spotlight. It is argued that animals' eyes are supposed to have different rod and cones structure from those found in the human eye, and the idea is that the lamper can shine the beam of light around the field, see the rabbit without the rabbit seeing him and thus be able to get up close to his rabbit before removing the filter and letting the dog see the prey. It may work – I'm no biologist, so I can't be certain as to whether rabbits can see this diffused red light. I've tried this device and it worked well, allowing me to get up close to the rabbits without the dog seeing the quarry. After a while however the lurchers seem to be able to pick out rabbits even in the red beam so it seems logical that after a while rabbits will also be able to see the red beam of light. Certainly some areas, particularly around the motorways, are lamped very regularly and rabbits are so used to the lamp and the dangers it brings that they bolt for home immediately a light is played on them; whereas rabbits which rarely see a lamper will usually allow a lamper to get quite close to them before bolting.

A great variety of lamps are available to the sportsman, and I am grateful to Doug Cooper of C.T.F. for his help concerning the details of proprietary brands of night hunting equipment. Many firms make up a simple lamping kit of the type I've just described using 12 volt batteries and spotlight. These pieces of equipment are professionally made and subsequently are less likely to go wrong at times when the lamper can least afford them to. Generally these lamping kit batteries are sold protected by well made wooden boxes which are usually either very tightly fitting or padded to prevent damage to the battery. Although such kits may appear to be expensive when compared to the scrapyard gleaned kit, they are nevertheless cheaper than home made kits put together with new material simply because the makers of these kits usually get very good trade discounts on the batteries and lights used and therefore are able to make their products cheaply enough to attract customers. Such lamping kits are relatively simple to operate and maintain and make a good purchase for the lamper just starting out.

At the time of writing there are an enormous number of lamps, and lamping kits available to the public. One of the most reliable is the Swinford Night Lamp, a box-like contraption which needs very little maintenance and has a built in charge so that all the exhausted lamper has to do when he returns after a night's hunting is to plug the battery into the mains. The beams are exceedingly powerful, throwing a light of between 45,000–55,000 candle power. However, this type of lamp has one great disadvantage. Not only is the lamp bulky but the box-like shape doesn't lend itself to the mobility needed by a lamper working a dog with the beam. I wrote a criticism of this type of lamp only recently and mentioned that it was almost impossible to manipulate this type of lamp to follow a running rabbit with this shape of lamping device. My article obviously caused some offence (most of my articles do!) for I received a batch of angry letters, one of which was written by a man from Stafford who invited me out to watch him use the Swinford Night Lamp. I journeyed to Stafford in early November and watched my critic use the lamp. I confess I still found the box-shaped piece of equipment cumbersome even after I was shown the knack of using one, but my new associate seemed to be able to throw the lamp around more like a conjuror than a lamper. Some people seem to get very good results with this type of lamp, but one cannot help but feel that Swinfords would do much better to modify the original design of the lamp and fit the box-like shape with a pistol grip to allow extra mobility.

Perhaps the most popular and serviceable type of lamp available to the night hunter is the Q beam and some of the Q beam variations such as the Q beam Black Max and the Q beam Blue Max. The Q beam is a pistol grip lamp which not only allows for great mobility but also gives an almost unbelievably bright beam, a beam which quite literally will light up a 20 acre field. Some of the poaching fraternity who wrote to me after my articles concerning this type of beam claim that this lamp is unsuitable for their activities because of the power of the beam – a beam which must be a dead give-away to any gamekeeper who lives within a mile or so from the field being lamped. Be that as it may, the beam is very popular and C.T.F. assure me it is one of their best selling lamps. The Q beam Blue Max is simply a variation on the Q beam but has a 200,000 candle power beam which throws a 'no scatter' beam and hence cuts through fog, mist, and rain. If anything this beam is an even better night hunting light than the Q beam, but is so powerful that some professed poachers do not use this type of beam. The Q beam Black Max is another variation on the Q beam and is in fact a marked improvement. The makers claim that its 300,000 candle power beam makes it the world's most powerful hand held lamp and that the spotlight is virtually glare free. Actually I've not only used the Q beam Black Max but I've also been on the receiving end of the beam and can therefore vouch for its brightness. I had lamped a farm on which I have permission to rabbit but had failed to notify the owners that I was coming that night. Subsequently when I switched on my beam I was greeted by an even more powerful spotlight which left me nearly blind for an hour afterwards. One poacher who wrote to me after the publication of my article on lamps and lamping made the comment that the very highly powered Black Max beam was used by a friend of his to dazzle a pursuing gamekeeper while the others of the party made their escape.

However, the Q beam is not without its faults as a piece of lamping equipment. The beam is exceedingly powerful and ordinary batteries are rapidly drained by a Q beam. When I tested this beam with an ordinary 12 volt battery I found that the battery had an active life of well under an hour, but a heavy duty car battery wielded by an enthusiastic friend of mine went an entire night without giving out. Doug Cooper of C.T.F. assures me that the batteries specially designed for Q beams (two linked batteries actually) give a much longer life, but I confess I have yet to test these batteries.

Having got a lamp and a suitable puppy, how do we start the puppy lamping? Most lampers who intend to use a lurcher only for lamping are decidedly careful about allowing a puppy a chance to course rabbits during the daylight hours. The reason for this is that no matter how well a puppy will try at a rabbit while hunting by day it's an odds-on shot that he will miss his rabbit; and when a puppy, or an adult for that matter, loses its rabbit, even the most sight hound bred hunting dog will put its nose down and endeavour to find its rabbit by hunting it up by nose. Two lampers from Burnley who write to me regularly refuse to allow a puppy to exercise in spots where there are enticing scents on the grass and generally never allow a puppy off the leash while it is exercising. While this does seem to me to be just a little extreme, their dogs, an unprepossessing mixture of Collie, Bedlington, whippet, greyhound and possibly deerhound (sold to them as straight greyhound/Saluki crosses!) certainly work exceedingly well and must be some of the best all-round lamp dogs I have yet to see. When the dogs miss a rabbit, and only *Exchange and Mart* wonder dogs don't, the lurchers flash back to their owners to be run again. Not once during the exhibition they put on for me in October 1983 did either dog show any inclination to hunt on. Hauls in Lancashire are quite low as lamping is now very common due to the unemployment in that area, and as one of the boys puts it, 'getting prosecuted is just an occupational hazard'. Cooper remarked in fact that since the depression, there has been an incredible increase in the sales of lamping equipment though I suspect that boredom rather than poverty has forced many Lancashire lads into lamping and poaching. In fact I'm a bit unsure as to whether people have ever poached simply because they were starving, and those tales about poaching representing a war between the classes doesn't stand up to scrutiny either. Poachers who sell the game they steal (and I'm afraid steal is the correct word according to the law) are literally doing it out of devilment, nothing more, nothing less. If the same poachers wanted to get a really profitable night's work, a brick through a shop window or an attack on a council rent collector would get a bigger bag of swag. Poaching is the way those who can't afford it get sport for themselves and their dogs. They don't represent a subculture as most national papers would have the public believe – that's just hog wash. Poachers are simply men and women out for a night's sport, with the dangers of getting caught and prosecuted lending a little spice to the evening's entertainment.

It's not my aim to dwell on the subject of poaching, but the subject has been given some fairly peculiar publicity by the national papers. The prosecution of two youngsters a few months ago found in possession of just one rabbit, but charged and convicted for possessing an offensive weapon – a skinning knife certainly seems a set up to me, with one of the magistrates with a bee in his bonnet about stopping poaching. No-one who goes out lamping rabbits, goes without a knife, but only one in a million would consider using the knife for anything other than gutting rabbits. Now anyone who gets his 'collar felt' while lamping simply throws his knife away as soon as he realizes that the game is up.

Starting a puppy lamping can be either very simple or very difficult, and that is not such a silly comment as it at first appears. Some puppies take to the sport very quickly, while others are slower and may take ages before the penny drops. One example comes to mind most readily. About ten years ago an associate of my father turned up at the yard with a really outstanding puppy, a black and white, collie-marked, rough-coated bitch looking as though someone had mated a line of collie bred lurchers with a dog with a decided dash of deerhound about it. It was the sort of lurcher I've always dreamed of, the sort of dog I could have put together if I'd been given the pieces of a million nearly perfect lurchers. The trouble was that in my opinion the beast had gone to the wrong person, the general dealer sort of lurcher owner, the sort of man who would sell any dog providing the price was right. He'd paid seven pounds for the puppy, or so he boasted, but when I offered him twenty for it, he sensed its value and refused to sell. So I did the only thing I could – for I had fallen in love with the bitch. I offered to train the bitch for the traveller, and he nearly broke my hand off accepting the deal. I had quite a bad time breaking her to the lead, for the traveller had let the bitch go too long without training. Eventually I decided to start her to rabbit by lamping her, for it is usually easier to start a lurcher to rabbit when the rabbit is being lamped. The first night we ventured out the conditions couldn't have been better: the night was as black as a crow's wing, there was a high wind and a very light drizzle. If I'd dreamed up such a night, I couldn't have asked for more. The dog on the leash was straining for action, and there were so many rabbits in the field that I was spoilt for choice. I walked up to one and it squatted, refusing to move even though both the dog and I walked right up to it and if I'd wanted to I could have reached down and picked it up for the dog didn't see it, and though I fixed it in the beam for ages before it moved, there was no way the lurcher would look at it. It just didn't seem to realize that it must look down the beam to see the rabbit and try as I might I couldn't persuade it to follow the light. I yanked the lead, moved the beam to stir the rabbit and finally resorted to pushing the bitch's head down to the squatting rabbit more in desperation than hope. There was no way I could get her to show even an interest in the beam of light and after thirty fruitless attempts which put every rabbit back to cover, I returned home, the bitch no wiser for the night's adventure. I've had this happen before and the penny soon drops, but in this case the penny was to take quite a long time to fall. I walked up maybe a hundred rabbits in the next few weeks, absolute sitters which wouldn't have been beyond the capabilities of a cripple to take, yet not once did the bitch realize that I was shining the light to illuminate the rabbit. A month later, she cottoned on to what I was trying to do and never looked back. She stayed another three months with me, became a brilliant lamper and I felt quite sick when the traveller asked me to return her. I tried to buy her, offering a ridiculously high price considering that he'd paid seven pounds for her, and I'd spent several months training her but he wouldn't hear of it. He returned to drop off a load of scrap about six months later and I asked him about the bitch. His son had sold it for £10 at Appleby Fair!

Some puppies take to the game immediately however, particularly if one can allow the youngster a chance to watch an old dog run a rabbit in the beam, but it doesn't necessarily follow that because a dog picks up the sport quickly that he will be a first class lamper. There is many a slip between starting a quick-learning lamper and finishing up with a top grade animal. Half the skill of lamping is blending into the ways of the dog one has trained, getting to know and understand his little quirks while he gets to know yours. Many outstanding lamping dogs get to learn certain tricks of the trade for themselves. Some develop the knack of picking up the rabbit without changing stride, a spectacular piece of work to watch. Others learn to cut off the rabbit by getting between the warrens and the rabbit, a skill a dog acquires most readily if one lamps the same places regularly. Sadly, others learn to take a rabbit by using a flying rugby tackle, a piece of catching which might look spectacular but has a fairly devasting effect on the carcass of the rabbit and often renders it not only unsaleable, but quite frequently uneatable; but I've reserved the subject of hard mouth for another chapter.

Now, however, seems a good time to expose the teller of tall tales. Six months ago I bred a nice litter of Bedlington/greyhound puppies mating a rather tall greyhound to a very game but very small Bedlington terrier male bred by Miss Margaret Williamson of Neath, and advertised them in *Exchange and Mart*. In Birmingham we have a special term for first rate idiots: we call them Wallys. Believe me, there are some 100 per cent pure Wallys keeping lurchers, and an advert in *Exchange and Mart* brings them all out of the woodwork. A vendor of lurchers must expect a fair share of challengers, irate overgrown schoolboys who want to boost their own egos by phoning up someone and challenging them to a coursing contest – this is a breed of idiot that abounds among lurchermen – but the sort that really 'bugs' me is the 'guarantee merchant' who usually begins his phone call with 'Can you guarantee your puppy will take three out of four hares?' or in the case of my advertisement, which clearly specified that the litter were bred for lamping, 'Can you guarantee this puppy will take twenty rabbits a night?' The newcomer to this sport must at all costs turn a deaf ear to the idiot who haunts almost every show claiming that their dogs regularly knock down fifty rabbits a night. Indeed, a dog which regularly takes twenty rabbits a night is a bit of a wonder dog. Take a good look at the tale and throw in a sprinkling of common sense to see how the brew gels. If a man took twenty rabbits every night of the year he'd be taking upwards of 7,000 rabbits a year. Most of the year rabbits are unsuitable for sale partly because no-one buys rabbits in the summer and partly because most does are pregnant at that time. Next, a haul of twenty rabbits a night would require an enormous area of rabbit-rich ground, and last but certainly not least, a single dog which catches twenty rabbits a night has, unless the conditions are always ideal, run between forty and sixty rabbits to get such a haul, for although there are hundreds of 'this dog never misses lurchers' offered for sale, I've never seen one, and one out of two as a ratio of catches to rabbits run is a pretty fair average. So let's assume that the dog tries for say 60 rabbits a night and each rabbit runs perhaps 200 yards. Thus a dog is going to have to run 12,000 yards a night at 30 mph which is not all that much short of seven miles. Believe me, a dog is tested somewhat taking around 20 rabbits a night, let alone an odd hare or so thrown in for good measure.

Hares are not all that difficult to take on the beam and I've taken lamped hares with lurchers which wouldn't have had a chance of catching hare run by day. Hares are taken by most lamping lurchers from time to time and I once knew a whippet which became so canny that she wouldn't look at a hare which got up by day, but she caught many by night. There are knacks regarding taking hares on the lamp, the oldest one of which is if one runs a hare into a hedge, keep the lamp on the hedge and the chances are the hare will come back out; it doesn't always work but sometimes it will. However a run on hare by lamplight is nowhere near as spectacular as a run by daylight, though it can be every bit as exhausting for the dog, which of course brings us to the subject of whether or not hares are actually worth lamping, and frankly I don't think they are. At the time of writing a hare peddled around the pubs or sold on a market stall fetches about £2.50 give or take fifty pence, and a hare is not everyone's choice of meat. It is tough, invariably very strong tasting, and the quantity of meat a hare provides is a bit much for the average 2.4 kids family. Not everyone fancies hares, and they are often quite difficult to sell, for the majority of the public don't want the fuss (and smell) of hanging the beast, marinating it in wine or cider and then being stuck with a large quantity of strong-smelling and strong-tasting meat. During war time years things were different, and hares found a ready market during the times of meat rationing. These days they are quite hard to sell. Rabbits, however, seem to be coming back into fashion. Ten years ago, with the horrors of myxomatosis still in their minds the general public wouldn't eat rabbit meat. These days they are importing boatloads of rabbit from China. British rabbits caught by lurchers, shot or ferreted fetch a pound a piece in pubs or to private customers. So, before the lamper considers slipping his dog on a hare he should consider how much effort and time his dog is likely to expend bringing down a hare and whether the £2.50 for the hare is worth the effort. I came to the conclusion that it wasn't some five years ago when I was lamping some medium sized fields in Hereford, using just one dog. From the point of view of the night affording the right conditions for lamping I couldn't ask for more, but there were few rabbits present and the area had been lamped so often those rabbits sitting out were hugging the hedges. I was about to cry 'Quit' and go home when a large jack hare got up in the beam and I slipped the dog. He had had five fruitless runs and two catches at the time so he was moderately fresh and in good shape, but the hare had fair to good 'law' and it took some doing to turn him. As it was it turned out to be one of the most exhausting runs I've ever seen and as the dog retrieved the hare to hand I realized his lungs must have felt like the inside of a blast furnace and I was convinced he was not capable of another run that night. As I hopped back across the fences I shone the lamp into a field adjacent to the ones I had lamped. The place was alive with 'sitters', way out in the field, just waiting to be nabbed. I looked down at the exhausted dog, listened to his sobbing panting, and decided not to chance it. The hare turned out to be so badly crushed I couldn't sell it and the two rabbits were sold before I reached Birmingham. Since then I have not bothered to run hares, except when I have been invited out specifically to thin them out.

On the subject of knowing when a dog has had enough, it would be fair to say that many lurchermen simply don't give their dogs a break. To take a dog out of its kennel only for a walk, and then to expect it to put up a good show against a hare is rather like fetching Sebastian Coe back from his holiday and then without warning entering him against the top milers of the world. Running dogs with a fair proportion of greyhound blood in their make up will usually try until they drop but running them unfit is not only unfair, but damnably cruel. Over-running them, not packing up and going home when the dog is becoming weary, is not only a bit savage, but counter-productive. Some dogs will be visibly blowing when they've had enough, but others will try until they die of heart failure and yet give little indication that things are not going well. Many Saluki-bred lurchers don't pant even after hard runs, but as soon as the dog looks jaded or puts in a series of feeble efforts against rabbits it should take without any trouble, it is time to think about going home. One more run could be the last straw which breaks the camel's back, as in the following tale. Some three or four years ago two of our local idiots, with more money than sense, saw an advert for an adult collie greyhound bitch in *Exchange and Mart*. After phoning the seller they went across to see the bitch, which was not looking her best as she'd just aborted her litter. So these two donkeys took her round several lurchermen to get a second opinion. The opinions must have been favourable for they brought the bitch who was not only discharging badly, but also heavy with milk. Several of us warned them that she was in no condition to run, but our advice fell on deaf ears, for the night of the purchase they were off running a particularly heavily-keepered estate known locally as 'The Forbidden Land'. The bitch had a reputation of being a tryer but even the gutsiest of bitches just won't do well when they've aborted and are heavy with milk. The upshot of the matter was that they ran her and ran her long after they should have cried stop, and she simply collapsed and died on one of the fields in The Forbidden Land. That evening they visited all the lurchermen who had advised on the purchase and created Hell because we'd advised them to buy a 'duff dog'! A penny for all the lurchers killed or crippled by idiots would easily clear the national debt, and since then I've never advised anyone on the purchase of an adult or a puppy. I was told by a keeper who lives fifteen miles from my home that scarcely a week goes by summer or winter when he doesn't find a dead, dying or crippled lurcher on his fields. So forget the tales of bottomless stamina one hears from idiots at the shows, and rest your lurcher if he shows he's tiring or better still pick him up and go home.

Taking foxes with a beam of light is a very emotive subject at the time of writing, with the field sport purists throwing up their hands in horror at the thought of a fox being killed by a lurcher, though the self-same people would condone fox hounds dismembering the same fox. D. B. Plummer's *The Complete Lurcher* received an adverse criticism in *Shooting Times* because it contained a chapter on lamping foxes. The reviewer hit the book rather fiercely because of the fox hunting chapter and then enjoyed anonymity by signing his name 'Courser'. To this day no-one has owned up to writing that criticism.

Personally I don't see any wrong in lamping foxes and selling the skins to furriers and either feeding the skinned carcasses to ferrets or to Chinese restaurants, for these places will pay as much as six pounds a carcass for a fox. I don't hunt fox because my lurchers aren't really interested in foxes and I've never taken the trouble to enter them. The majority of lurchers will try for a fox and even bowl one, but it requires a rather different type of dog to kill one. Once again may I quote David Hancock of Sutton Coldfield, who specializes in breeding certain dogs for fox catching.

> Some dogs are natural fox catchers and enter to a fox without any encouragement. If such a dog gets a nip for their troubles during the first encounter, so much the better as it sharpens them up for the job. Others need to be entered carefully, either by ragging a dead fox and encouraging the lurcher to worry the carcass or better still restraining them while they watch a seasoned fox-killer at work and then slipping the youngster on the dead fox. Others simply don't want to know fox and no coaxing or encouragement will get them to catch foxes. Size is no indication of the merits of a dog, although a well-built powerful lurcher will usually wind a fox on the first lunge and the rest will

come easily. What counts, though, is not the muscle but the courage of the dog and quite slender bitches are often as good at killing foxes as large powerful males. It's also complete and utter rubbish that working a dog at a fox every now and then ruins them for retrieving unmarked rabbits. Lurchers know when a creature is going to bite them and they'll try and finish the fox before it does. They are also aware of the fact that a rabbit won't harm them, and they don't bother to kill a creature which isn't going to put up a fight. Lamping foxes, calling them in close with rabbit squeaks, is the easiest way of catching them. I've found the most suitable dogs for fox-killing are three-quarter bred collie greyhounds bred by mating a really hard collie greyhound to a good class coursing bitch which has seen quite a lot of action on the coursing field. If the dam has shown an interest or has killed foxes, so much the better, for breeding is half the battle where fox-catching lurchers are concerned. Puppies shouldn't be tried to fox until they have experience at picking up other quarry and while it must be admitted that most lurchers can outpace a fox – it's a very poor lurcher that can't – catching and killing a fox is another matter and requires a dog with specialised skills and a rather mean mental attitude.

18 *Hard Mouth*

The ownership of a hard-mouthed dog is the curse of all lurcher owners and perhaps it is only right to define exactly what is meant by a hard mouth. A dog possessing a soft mouth tends to retrieve its catch alive and often unharmed: a hard-mouthed dog is a dog which mangles its prey, bruising the flesh, piercing the skin, and sometimes crushing the bones of its catch. A hard-mouthed lurcher may be just dandy for the man who enjoys coursing and doesn't want to eat his lurcher's catch, but for the pot-hunter or those who want to sell their catch a hard-mouthed dog is a liability. As to how common hard mouths are in the lurcher world, a trip to the local market and the examination of rabbits brought in by lampers will convince the reader how many lurchers are hard-mouthed. At the market where I sometimes sell my catch I checked the other rabbits handed in by lampers and found well over a quarter very badly bruised and frankly not really edible, and I must stress our market is no exception to the rule.

What are the causes of such a problem? It is a problem which halves the value of any coursing dog and reduces the selling price of a hitherto good lamping dog to absolute zero. A popular misconception concerning the development of hard mouths is that such dogs learn their habits in the nest and one should not get a puppy involved in rough play or tug of war games in case it develops a tendency to rag and damage its prey later on in life. Personally I believe this is absolute rubbish, though little one says influences many Midland lamping men who treat their puppies in a very staid and serious manner in order, so they believe, to prevent hard mouths. To these I say go to a breeder of track whippets and ask how a puppy is trained. Puppies are allowed to play, to rip, to tear at any rags they see, and socks, straps of linen and so on are thrown in to them to get them interested. Many of these cast whippets, dogs too big or too old for racing, find homes with rabbit hunters and very few of these cast whippets become hard mouthed. In fact I actually saw one of these whippets run in Shropshire and not only was it one of the very few whippets I've seen that was capable of single-handed hare catching, it is the only dog I've ever seen pick up a live hare and retrieve it not only live, but unmarked to hand.

This brings us to what I consider to be the principal cause of hard mouth in lurchers, namely, excessive running of hares. I am probably very prejudiced about this as I am not a habitual hare courser, and thus my views regarding the development of a hard mouth are shaped by this. Hares are powerful creatures and it is as much as a grown man can do to handle one. My father tells me that during the balmy days between World War I and II the farm labourers in the Cotswolds were a delightfully rustic band of men given to pranks and jokes which may be considered childish today but were acceptable during the days when folk were unspoilt by television and sophistication. Every harvest time all the villagers would watch as the harvester went round and round the field until only a small patch of corn was left. The children and adults alike would then shout 'The rabbits are coming out' and leap into the standing corn to grab a rabbit or so. Gamer young bucks of the village would make a lunge for a hare and attempt to hold it alive. As most of the young men were naked to the waist during the corn cutting it was not uncommon to find some of the hare catchers very badly scratched for their efforts.

To me it seems logical that dogs which run hares regularly are also at a bit of a loss as to what to do when a hare is caught and not only begins to scream blue murder but also fights like a wild cat. Dogs will invariably kill such a creature quickly to prevent damage to themselves, and thus I believe is born the failing known as hard mouth. This opinion is by no means totally accepted by all. In October 1983 an article of mine concerning the subject of hard mouth, its cause and cures, was published in *Shooting News* in answer to a man who wrote asking the reasons for the development of the habit. The article received a certain amount of acclaim but also quite a lot of criticism. D. B. Plummer had this to say about my belief that frequent work on hares caused a lurcher to develop a hard mouth:

> Much as I enjoy your articles and your 'different' style of writing, I cannot agree with your assumption that a hard mouth is caused by the regular use of the lurcher for hare catching. Few hares are retrieved alive, but fewer still are killed on the point of impact between dog and prey. A dog strikes at the hare, catches it, and only when the hare begins to struggle fiercely does the dog stop its violent kicking by increasing the pressure of the bite. A rabbit so taken, rarely offers up such a struggle and thus the dog has no need to put in the finishing bite. Thus many dogs which will shake a fox to death in minutes will also retrieve a rabbit alive and unbruised to hand. The fact that many of famous hare killing dogs are hard mouthed is not due to the fact that they transfer the hare killing bite to captured rabbits, but quite simply

99

because, to get the maximum speed from a strain of coursing lurcher, massive infusions of greyhound blood are added to an already sight hound saturated mix, and the resulting long dogs are invariably hard mouthed due to the use of certain notoriously hard strains of coursing greyhound used in their creation.

I must hasten to add that, while it has to be admitted that Plummer is the most 'thinking' of today's sporting writers and has an enormous following, he is not inevitably correct because of this.

Yet it has to be admitted that certain strains of lurcher are rat-trap mouthed and never return anything unmarked, that is when those dogs decide to retrieve at all. The formidable strains of Saluki/greyhound bred around Hertfordshire are renowned hare killers, amongst the best I've seen in fact, derived as they are from a dog bred from an imported family of smooth-coated Salukis (very different in appearance from their longer coated cousins but winners in the field) and some top class coursing greyhounds. As hare killers these dogs are knockouts with speed and stamina to spare. The majority of the dogs of travellers around that area are from this family. I quote Greg Peters who wrote to me after what he considered to be a derogatory article on the Saluki/greyhound:

> The best hare coursing dogs for twenty or thirty miles around London are owned by a settled Romany family called the Stanley brothers. These are wonderful hare killers equal to any dogs in the world. I own one of these dogs and he is unbeaten in the best of three contests. The family are as a rule very hard mouthed but are used exclusively for competitive coursing.

But breeding alone cannot be responsible for the rash of hard mouths some modern lurchers seem to have. The practice of running two or more dogs at lamped rabbits is madness and not only is a collision with catastrophic results inevitable, but a damaged carcass is the result of a two-way catch. I spent a very interesting night lamping near Ashby with a chap who wrote to me inviting me up for the weekend. His hospitality was incredible, but the sight of his five deerhoundy lurchers running at once at a lamped rabbit is the part I shall remember most about the evening. Dogs are invariably jealous of each other's catches and hence when a rabbit is caught by one, the other is bound to pitch in and seize the prize. The outcome is predictable – a very long, stretched, unsaleable rabbit fit only for ferret food or a dummy to train a puppy.

However, even the presence of another dog behind the lamp, even if that dog is on a slip, is often enough to start the problem of hard mouth. As I have just mentioned, jealousy between two dogs, even dogs owned by the same person is intense; and jealousy between hunting dogs is one of the reasons why track greyhounds try so hard to catch a clockwork hare. Hence a dog returning proudly, head high, rabbit in mouth, only to be greeted by the lunging of another dog behind the lamp eager to snatch up the rabbit, is likely to cause the dog with the rabbit to walk around the lamper for a while, even refusing to give up its rabbit when approached by the owner. The answer to this problem is obvious. Leave the other dog in the van while you lamp the first dog and appealing as the idea may be of running dogs in relays to prevent a dog getting worn out, don't do it. Remember that a dog walking round and round the lamper, its jaws tightening on its prey by the second, is not only going to mangle the carcass beyond recognition, but is also going to put every feeding rabbit back in the warrens through the commotion you and the lurcher are causing.

However if you really do want a whole haul of damaged rabbits fit only to feed hungry ferrets, and you are hell-bent on producing a ruined hard mouthed dog whose catches look as if a crocodile rather than a lurcher has retrieved them, I know of a certain way. Watch your lurcher carefully as the night progresses and, as he tires, put in a few extra and even unnecessary runs. If the dog looks very tired run him even harder and, hey presto, in next to no time the rabbits the dog fetches back will have pierced ribs, and very bruised bowels, unsaleable even in the darkest corner of a pub. The reason for the dog developing this habit, a habit which if allowed to develop even further makes the dog's value plummet to zero, is that as the dog becomes more and more tired, the effort of carrying a struggling rabbit back to hand becomes greater and greater; so the dog tightens its grip to finish off the rabbit to prevent further hassle when retrieving a rabbit and kills it before fetching it to hand.

Other dogs develop an odd method of catching rabbits, and this can cause quite a lot of damage to the carcass. Beware of spectacular catches, the sort of 'Hell, no other dog could have taken that rabbit' type of catches. I refer to the rolling somersault, coming up with 'rabbit in mouth' type of catch, which looks spectacular indeed, but does the rabbit in its mouth no good at all. Some dogs will continue to catch in this manner, and there is little one can do except switch off the beam and get the dog back every time a rabbit looks like getting in a spot which only the dog's flying tackle will ensure the rabbit is caught. It's not a good habit to develop: I've owned a dog who looked as though he belonged in a circus rather than on a coursing field and came by him in a most unusual manner. I've nothing against tinkers, didicais and travellers generally; I've known them all my life and I've been around enough to know that there are good and bad in every race or creed under the sun. Some of the people I've met have been good to me while others have 'done me dirt' so I take people as they come. But I'm usually a bit reluctant to buy an adult dog from one, simply because many of their lurchers have the marks of living a bit rough. One day a wagonload of scrap was driven into the yard by a wizened, scarred man of maybe fifty, his equally weatherworn wife who in addition to a lined face had a mouthful of multicoloured teeth and an ugly scrawny youth at her side. With them they had a medium sized lurcher bitch, smooth coated, with no particular class or type about her, but a bitch which looked a worker nevertheless. If I had to bet on her breeding, I'd have said that someone had mated a rather mongrelly lurcher bitch to a good class three-quarter bred collie stud. She was nothing to look at, but had the sort of sparkle that all good working lurchers seem to have, an indescribable brightness that only needs exploiting to get the best out of her. The lad played with her in the yard, bouncing a rubber ball and getting her to catch the ball in mid-air. She was a born acrobat, as much a circus dog as a hunter, and I paid no more attention to her, but the lad had noticed the interest I'd shown and in a few days he was back with her. The old man had been picked up by the police for stealing a load of copper fittings, and as the old man was as the law puts it 'of no fixed abode', the bench refused to grant bail and kept the old chap in custody. The lad said that the bitch was a bit much for the old lady and he wanted to sell her. I paid a fiver for her, though I didn't really want her. However I suppose I'm a sucker for a bargain of any sort – a quality that's bred in the bone, I suppose, for Dad had the same failings. She learned the lamp easily, and I've never met a traveller who uses a dog on a lamp, possibly because no real traveller has the opportunity to change batteries regularly. However, although she caught rabbits easily, her acrobatics made her a liability, for she bruised every rabbit she took. I kept her a year maybe, until she broke her neck somersaulting into a ditch full of old junk.

How to *cure* a hard mouth is another matter for prevention is not only better than cure in this case, it is in fact the only way, for it is impossible to cure a dog which develops the irritating habit. The cures suggested by many lurcher men, putting barbed wire inside a dead rabbit's skin, is a method only likely to prevent the lurcher retrieving, rather than stopping hard mouth.

19 *Opening Up*

Opening up, giving tongue when chasing or quite simply barking as quarry tries to escape, is supposedly the reason why there are a great number of lurchers changing hands every day. Next to mangling quarry, refusing to chase or an inability to pick up running rabbits or hares, opening up is the most heinous fault a lurcher can manifest.

Not only is opening up irritating – for a barking dog certainly does upset a coursing party – but a dog which expends its energy barking while it courses is less likely to catch its prey than a dog which runs silently. Furthermore, a lamping lurcher which opens up as it runs tends to put every rabbit on the field back to ground. Last, but certainly not least, the average lurcherman tends to frequent places where he is seldom invited and a barking dog is certainly a liability on these places.

As to what causes opening up, there have been a spate of articles and letters concerning the subject in the sporting press recently, but most of the theories put forward do not hold water when examined carefully.

Several theories are offered as to why a dog 'opens up' when coursing. Most pure bred sight hounds, greyhounds, deerhounds, Salukis, Afghans, and Borzois seldom bark when coursing, so perhaps the answer lies with the base stock which is mated to greyhounds and so on to produce lurchers. Conversely, several strains of whippet, both coursing and racing strains, are notoriously yappy when coursing and some of the most vocal dogs I've ever seen have been hybrid whippet greyhounds. Bedlington lurchers are also reputed to be vociferous when pursuing quarry, supposedly due to the fact that Bedlingtons are terriers and terriers are required to bay at quarry below ground. Bedlington terriers however have a reputation for being mute below ground, and hence it is unlikely that Bedlington crosses are any more likely to open up than other lurchers.

However, one of the main causes of opening up is very obvious. If a puppy is overmatched with its quarry because the puppy is really too young to be attempting such a course, or because the quarry is far too strong to give the puppy a chance to catch it, there is a tendency for the puppy to begin to bark at the escaping rabbit or hare in

103

exasperation. For this reason the puppyhood of a lurcher should be spent developing muscle and developing an affinity with the owner, rather than making fruitless and damaging attempts to catch rabbits. First tries at rabbits should be easy slips with at least some chance of the lurcher making a catch.

Once a lurcher has started yapping as it chases, there is literally nothing the lurcherman can do to stop it. Debarking a dog is perhaps a little drastic and also more than just a little expensive, though a valuable lurcher which has just developed this habit may be worth the expense of the operation to sever its vocal chords. Far too many lurchermen tend to sell a puppy as soon as it begins to yap, and this is a mistake. Perhaps the very nature of lurcher owners makes them change dogs often and for very little cause. Very often puppies which make or or two mistakes are simply passed on by their disgruntled owners, who find all too late perhaps that the baby has outgrown its infantile ways and has become a first class worker. Puppies should be given a chance, and if a youngster does put in a yap or so while running, for goodness sake have patience with him, and don't up and sell the dog at the first chance. One swallow doesn't make a summer, and likewise one yap doesn't make a puppy guilty of being a lurcher which opens up.

20 *Coursing*

If I might recap at this point, the lurcher or bastard greyhound was bred or perhaps came into existence to be a potfiller, the dog of the meat-hungry farm worker, as entertaining to keep as it was useful. It was not designed as a dog to compete in contests involving the pursuit and capture of hares under the rules and regulations. The original lurcher, the collie adulterated with greyhound blood may have picked up the occasional hare for the pot, but these hares were usually obtained by a dog running free, taking its hare by stealth more than speed, allowing it little or no law and chasing it over country the dog knew almost as well as the hare.

Greyhounds, on the other hand, have been kept for centuries to chase and bring down hares and deer rather than rabbits and game birds and have been selectively bred to have breathtaking bursts of speed and a phenomenal inbuilt knowledge of the ways of the hare. Salukis, too (perhaps more than greyhounds) have been bred for hare coursing, and the number of hares a good Saluki will pull down on suitable coursing land is rather amazing. A lurcherman who believes that the lurcher or longdog he has in his possession will knock spots off any coursing greyhound or coursing Saluki might do well to visit a typical greyhound or better still coursing Saluki meet. I have to admit I consider myself no expert either on Salukis or greyhounds, but I've attended numerous coursing meetings involving greyhounds, Salukis and lurchers and I have to admit I've yet to see a lurcher hold a candle to a good experienced Saluki as a catcher of hares. Admittedly the spectator is unlikely to see examples of dogs hunting up quarry, and even less likely to see a retrieve of any sort. Furthermore the faraway look, and slowness to respond to command of any sort which characterize Salukis would not appeal to the average lurcher coursing man, but if the reader would like to obtain a dog to chase hares then he would do well to go to a breeder of a good strain of Saluki, preferably one which has a good dash of imported blood in its veins. This blood should be obtained for preference from Saudi Arabia rather than from Iran, for Iranian dogs are run on wolf, boar and sometimes leopard as well as hare, whereas the Saudi Arabian hounds are now kept almost exclusively for hare, now that the gazelle has become an endangered species in that country. Some of the Saudi imports I've seen are scarcely heavier than a really tall whippet, but as hare catchers (and only hare catchers, I must add) they are unbeatable. At one meet I attended I watched one imported dog run course after course – hard grinding courses at that – and it still finished the day looking as though it had not exerted itself. It killed eleven hares that day, admittedly running with other dogs, but eleven hares given fair law would be beyond the catching ability of most lurchers.

Twenty years ago I found very little trouble obtaining permission to course hares on other people's land. Now even friends of my father seem reluctant to have anyone with lurchers running on their land. A destructive element has entered the world of lurchermen, an element light years away from the village poacher, the scallywag everyone tolerated although they knew he took the occasional hare or rabbit from the land. A particularly nasty type of person seems to have got in on the lurcher scene these days, louts who are not only destructive and disrespectful to landowners (a modicum of respect goes a long way regarding securing a good piece of ground for hare coursing) but also decidedly vicious to livestock and, to cap it all, thieves who are not averse to killing a sheep or two if the mood suits them. A matter of eight months ago I visited an old friend of my father's who owns a piece of land on the edges of Cannock Chase, a vast patch of forestry commission land near the M6, and an area noted for its stock of deer. I had hunted this land for four or five years not only with permission but also with a great deal of cordial welcome with tea and cakes in exchange for the odd rabbit which I took on the land. When I arrived there last time I was greeted less cordially. The landowner had been visited by a band of very plausible lads from Castle Bromwich who not only convinced him that they'd do no damage to his property, but that they'd lend a hand, free of charge at harvest time. He allowed them to course his land and in return they not only broke fences, stole eggs, pulled parts from standing farm machinery to sell for scrap, but also put a crossbow bolt in one of his cattle, a bolt which pierced the gut; and it took the vet all his skill to pull the heifer through. The lads had used his farm as a jumping off spot to poach deer and the heifer had received the bolt either by mistake or more likely out of pique when the idiot band had experienced a dead day for deer. I still hunt the land, but it took all my powers of persuasion to convince him I wasn't of a similar mould to my predecessors.

Coursing land with enough hares to justify a day's work for a pair of good lurchers is hard to come by. Really outstanding places, places so thick with hares that (to quote Old Boothby) one had to take a hare

A hare in top gear. Running for its life

out of the field to make space enough to put a dog in, are snapped up by greyhound and Saluki coursing clubs. These clubs jealously protect the land they have hired for coursing meets and any unauthorized persons venturing on the land are usually prosecuted or worse. Worse needs explanation, I think. The really coveted piece of coursing land called 'The Forbidden Land' by our local lunatic lurcher element is keepered by two ex-fighters, gigantic men, with little sense of value where life and limbs are concerned. Both are, so the tale goes, ex-poachers who know the ropes and so anyone venturing on their domain is in for a very bad time indeed. Tales of unpleasant accidents happening to lurchermen and their dogs abound, though stories of men being prosecuted for poaching that estate are practically non-existent. One of the keepers, aware of the ways hares run, once nailed a piece of very strong piano wire between two gate posts as tightly as a guitar string and at just the right height so as to decapitate a lurcher as it passes through the gate. Other tales are of silent vengeance wreaked on lurchers illuminated in the lamp just long enough for a .22 rifle fitted with a silencer to get a shot in. Keepers of this sort rarely prosecute and merely shoot the dog. A prosecution means a fine, so trivial that most poachers would laugh at it, whereas a dog shot means at least a six or seven months layoff.

Nevertheless it is still possible to rent coursing ground. Our own local coursing club, a band of maybe five lurchermen, hire a day's coursing permission in Leicestershire and while the hares are certainly not numerous the owner of the property doesn't place any limit on the number of hares one takes there. The land is very open with miles of arable land enclosed by very high dry stone walls – perfect hare country, too perfect in fact for the hares are seldom caught on this estate. A variety of people also course this land, one of whom owns a pair of gigantic Irish wolfhounds – certainly not my sort of dog but all the same they put in some fairly strenuous, though fruitless courses after hares. The owner of these dogs told me that he's been going there once a week for five years and while he admits he has only caught one hare he doesn't seem particularly bothered about the absence of catches. I learn a lot from talking to such people and was surprised to learn that, up to a few years ago there was actually a club which catered for people who wished to course these huge Irish wolfhounds.

Obviously Irish wolfhounds are not the ideal dogs to course hares, for they are far too big and cumbersome. The best coursing dogs are greyhounds and Salukis and the best hybrids for the job, if coursing is one's pleasure, are longdog hybrids – rather brainless mixes of Saluki and greyhound for preference, dogs and bitches which level out at maybe 24–26 inches at the shoulder, with greyhound thrust and the Saluki's stamina. The enormous deerhound crosses look particularly good in the show ring, but most are far too tall to pick up hares, though most are very fast and burn up the ground between the slip and the first turn of the hare. On small fields a rather smaller lurcher comes into its own, a mix of whippet and greyhound, though today there are few legitimate breeders of this once much vaunted crossbred. The turning ability of this first cross is usually ideal, but they seldom prove effective on very large fields where a hare can really get its stride. Most Norfolk coursing men, in a country where the ground is very light because of its high peat content, and the fields very large, never use anything other than this Saluki crossbred. However these coursing dogs are not everyone's choice. Mick Douglas of Norfolk, who has achieved a great reputation as a coursing lurcher breeder used a hybrid collie lurcher called Rust as his original brood bitch and

mated her and her offspring to any top-class running dog winning best
of three hare killing contests in the Fens, will not consider using a stud
dog which has a trace of Saluki blood in its make up. Mick is a quiet
and reserved eccentric (he appeared as the bare-footed man on the
controversial programme *A Hunting Man*) and rarely leaves the Fens.
Doug Cooper of CTF however knows him well and says that Douglas
will not consider Saluki-bred stud dogs simply because the stock from
them is unpredictable. Some days Douglas says, they are literally
outstanding and will try like the devil on every hare that gets up in
front of them. On other days they show not only indifference, but also
apathy when asked to make a whole-hearted attempt at hare coursing.
Douglas has won many coursing contests against Saluki-bred longdogs simply because of this unpredictable nature, and as Fen-bred
travellers often bet considerable sums on these dogs, this capricious
nature could well mean an unpleasant end for these longdogs.

Others however swear by the cross as hare-killers and a lurcher
show in 'big country' such as the Fens and Salisbury Plains usually
sports a great number of these longdogs. Personally I find this cross no
more able than a pure-bred Saluki, though they do respond to training
a little better, and as to the capricious nature Douglas complains of,
few of the Stanleys who breed and run this crossbred would agree with
him.

More rubbish, unscientific nonsense and downright lies has been
talked about hares, than about any other creature, and it's worth a
visit to the beer tent at any lurcher show to listen to the tales. If every
story of a successful course at hare one hears in such places was true,
the hare would be extinct in Britain. There is scarcely a lurcherman
drinking in these tents who has not killed four or five hares a day and
all of them whoppers. If an onlooker who knew nothing of hares,
hunting, and lurchers overheard these conversations they would think
a hare was easy meat, prey for any cur to take whenever it wished.
Nothing could be further from the truth, for hares take some catching
and only the most fleet and agile of coursing dogs can bring one down.

Of course hares are taken by lurchers, longdogs and even whippets
and some dogs take them regularly. Likewise some dogs never seem to
be able to bring down a hare if the hare is given a sporting chance,
though many fairly slow lurchers kill them by stealth from time to
time. Hares are at their most vulnerable and easy to catch immediately
after the harvest, for when the corn is down and the fields are bare,
hares take some considerable time to adjust to the fact that the
cornfield is no longer a place to hide whenever danger threatens.
Likewise young hares, foolish and inexperienced in the ways of
running dogs, are not as difficult to catch as the older, wiser hares who

109

don't allow a dog to get near them, let alone course them. Hares run in September are therefore easier to catch than hares run in January, when they are at their strongest and more than a match for most dogs. A January coursing meet, particularly a coursing meet conducted on land where other meets have thinned out careless hares, are always hard and testing meets for lurchers, greyhounds or Salukis. Lurcher-men often scoff at the inability of many greyhounds running in the Waterloo cup to bring down their hares, but at the time when the Cup is run the Altcar hares, always famed for their strength and speed (indeed hares are deliberately encouraged and keepered at Altcar) are at their best, fit, strong, well fed and (judging from the number of Liverpool-based poachers) well used to the ways of running dogs.

For the idiot fringe among the lurcher fraternity – alas, an ever growing band – the coursing season never finishes for they hunt hares the year through, killing leverets scarcely able to run and worst of all killing pregnant does. This sort of action is not only stupid, wasteful and likely to reduce the hare population in a district to nil, but it is also food for the anti-brigade, and the League Against Cruel Sports rightly made a big issue out of a poacher who was convicted in 1981. The man, a thirty-five-year-old who should have known better, allowed his lurcher to chase a pregnant doe hare near to her time across a field, and the doe passed her leverets as she did so, frightened into premature parturition. This case was blown up out of all proportion by the press perhaps, but the man was fined a mere thirty pounds for 'trespassing in pursuit'.

Lurchers need not only to be sound in wind and limbs to catch hares but also well grown and mature, for a hare is a testing adversary. If the reader attends shows he will hear countless tales of puppies aged around six months which have caught hares, and some of these tales may be true. However the type of man who allows his puppy a chance to run a hare before the dog is old enough usually ruins the dog. About the time I bought my last Bedlington/greyhound puppy from Don Bakewell, an idiot associate who haunts my house asking advice but never heeding it, visited a Worcester-based lurcherman who is famed for dog dealing, trading dogs, swapping dogs and puppies and whose place must have housed just about every lurcher in the Midlands at some time. I showed the youth the puppy I bought and he phoned Don Bakewell about a puppy but by that time all the young stock had been sold. Straightaway the lad raced over to Worcestershire and bought himself a puppy, breeding unknown with maybe a dash of Bedlington, a hint of collie, more than a dash of whippet and a mite more besides. He brought his 'deerhound/greyhound' puppy across to show me and while it would never have passed muster in the light of the Trade Descriptions Act it was a fine puppy which would have made a good if not top-class working dog.

I took considerable time starting a puppy and as I confess I'm not in love with hare coursing, I start my puppy on a ferreted rabbit (more about that later) or on the lamp. My dog puppy was a gangly rather ugly creature at six months of age – Bedlington/greyhound hybrids go through an ugly stage in their development, whereas the other dog was just beginning to look like a rather classy lurcher. 'I'm trying him tomorrow,' he remarked, 'with so and so', a well known Midland lurcher ruiner who has maybe fifty dogs through his hands in a year. I advised against it, but my views on the matter fell on deaf ears and, as if to rub in what he considered to be my ignorance of lurchers, he brought a fairly well grown hare to the house the following evening. His puppy had taken it, he said, and henceforth day after day the lad took the puppy out after hares. By the time both our puppies were ten months of age; mine had outgrown its gawky ugly stage and was ready for starting. His on the other hand was parading around the shows with a 'For Sale' notice stuck around its neck. If I'd suggested the youth had gone to the local junior school and picked out a yongster to run against Sebastian Coe he would have thought I was quite mad. As it was he had done something very similar by putting a baby lurcher against some of the greatest athletes in the animal kingdom.

Eighteen months is not too old to try a lurcher to hare – and now the reader should be able to question the authenticity of those incredible *Exchange and Mart* advertisements which state that a dog is a first rate hare killer at eighteen months of age. In fact many longdogs are still very infantile at this age, and still grow into first rate hare catching dogs. E. G. Walsh says in *Lurchers And Longdogs* that lurchers kept exclusively for coursing should be kept off rabbits, but I fail to see why. Any quarry which sharpens a puppy without overtaxing him is useful and I have been asked by many coursing men to start twelve-month-old longdogs on lamped rabbits to gee them up for coursing. However Walsh's advice on starting a dog on hare is faultless. He recommends allowing a grown dog to run hard on the hare. This is an ideal way of starting a young dog as it has at least a chance against its opponent.

Joining a band of coursing supporters is fine, providing that the coursing is conducted under stringent rules. No more than two dogs should ever be slipped at a hare and I'm not all that sure that slipping two is a good idea. Running half a dozen dogs at a hare is madness and also counter-productive for fights invariably result from running dogs in number and injuries aplenty are usually the order of the day. Furthermore, the hare invariably gets away in the general chaos of the chase.

111

Never ever underestimate a hare, its speed, its stamina or indeed its ability to survive no matter how hard pressed the species might be. Biologists don't rate the hare as being a very intelligent creature as compared to a dog or a cat, but any lurcherman who has run hare regularly will tell you otherwise. Two years ago I was invited to a coursing meet in Atherstone, not an elaborate affair, just a friend out to show off a lurcher dog he had just bought from S. Wales, a very greyhoundy dog with muscle demarcation lines that would have put Charles Atlas to shame. It was a veritable power house of a dog and had cost my associate £500 (proving therefore he had more money than sense I thought at the time), but nevertheless it was a beautiful animal and had seen considerable work at hares from Margam to Cambridge. Personally I would have been reluctant to pay that sort of money for a coursing dog pure and simple, which wouldn't lamp and didn't know what its nose was for, but if the tales about it were only half-true it would have been worth watching. As it was we never did find out if the tales were true. We walked up on a hare, a perfect sitter who squatted and watched us approach almost indifferent to the dangers awaiting it. We slipped the dog giving a forty yard law, a reasonable distance for an unknown quantity even though the dog had a formidable record as a hare catcher. The dog was on it in a trice turning it in a matter of a hundred yards, coursing it back so close to us that I could have stuck out my foot and stopped it. Again and again the dog turned it until it struck out for a nearby ditch which contained a roll of pig wire through which the hare dashed time and time again. As it raced through the dog struck at it, missed or maybe even chopped the hare, for a squeal fit to wake the dead came from the wire, but the sound could have come from the dog as a loose strand of wire went straight through its eyeball piercing the skull. Many would have called this a coincidence, but there are so many coursing men who could tell similar stories of hares bringing good coursing dogs to grief that no hunter worth his salt sells the hare short brain wise. When hard pressed, hares seem to hang back until the dog seems to be able to put in a successful strike before flashing under a five bar gate, or disappearing up a drain pipe causing the dog to crack its skull against the bars of the gate or wreck its face against the glazed pipe of the drain. Hares will also take to water, swimming even fast-flowing rivers to escape from their pursuers and during one of the rare times I've been beagling, I've seen hares run under passing cars to throw off the pursuing pack. Thus any coursing man who sets out to take a hare would do well to remember it is not just a running machine but a quick-thinking little creature clever enough to be a match for any dog.

So great is the hare's running power that the lurcher owner is often apt to forget that his own dog is not made of steel and is apt to overrun him, running him too often on hares during a day's coursing. Lurchers with a high percentage of sight hound blood and longdogs particularly will try until they drop, for what such hybrids lack in sense they make up in heart, grit and sadly blind determination. Such dogs do not know when they've had enough and it is up to their owners to cry Halt to the day's coursing, when he considers the dog has had enough and not let the poor creature run itself to a state of exhaustion. The owner should watch for signs which indicate the dog has had more than enough and that all is not well. Watch how quickly the dog recovers from a testing and taxing run. If he takes longer and longer to cease panting, if he comes back head down, looking forlorn and beaten, if he doesn't look as if he's putting his all into each run at hare, stop, and stop immediately. Don't give him one last run or the course may well be a last run! Running dogs are made of the same tissue, the same flesh, bone and blood as other dogs and no matter how one rates the stamina of a dog, or more to the point no matter how much one has to prove to friends or those who claim to be friends, the owner must be able to say, 'I'm not going to run him again', in spite of the pleas and even taunts of people who are keen to see yet another run. More running dogs are killed or damaged because of the 'Just one more run' brigade than for any other reason, and most of the adult dogs capable of phenomenal coursing skills offered for sale in various sporting papers have been damaged by over-running on hare. Damage can manifest itself in various ways and in various degrees. Hard courses severely damage unfit dogs and stiffness, pulled and torn muscles can result from just one hard run, to continue when such injuries manifest themselves is not only stupid but also barbaric. Ruptured diaphragms and damaged hearts are usually present in the bands of lurchers which are regularly bought and sold throughout the country and anyone foolish enough to contemplate the purchase of a grown dog should get a vet's opinion before concluding the deal.

On the subject of idiots (and any book proffering advice to would-be lurcher men should contain a great deal on the habits of idiots) perhaps the most annoying type of idiot the coursing enthusiast is likely to meet is the 'challenger', the fool who has a sense of inadequacy that demands that he goes around challenging owners of running dogs to a coursing meet – against the idiot's present dog, and most idiots go through quite a few dogs in the space of a lifetime.

Very few of the idiots turn up to the coursing meets they have arranged to settle their imaginary differences with the people they have challenged, but those who do are the biggest liabilities. Few win any of the coursing events they have set up, most refuse to pay the bets they have made and quite a few will send friends to the property of the people whose dogs have outrun theirs and arrange to have the premises broken into and the dogs stolen. Lurcher thefts are very common at the time of writing; and, frankly, the police don't seem particularly worried as they take the attitude that one less poaching dog on their patch means less trouble for them. Don Southerd of Overseal, a famous Midlands coursing man who once challenged any owner of running dogs of any breed to compete with him in a best of three hares contest, used to course a fine brindled, box-headed dog of a formidable mix of Saluki/deerhound/greyhound and perhaps a dash of some type of Norfolk lurcher. Southerd, however, became too successful against the idiot brigade and the inevitable of course happened. To replace such a dog takes years and the tragedy is that dog thieves don't usually take too much care of the animals they have stolen.

Marking lurchers with one's own special code tatooed in the lurcher's ear as greyhounds are tatooed, is supposed to be a deterrent, though personally I find the whole business a waste of time. A professional lurcher thief, and there are several professionals at work in the country, will usually tatoo over the original marking or even cut off the ears of the unfortunate dog. Newcomers to the sport should realize that there are dozens of unsavoury characters in the lurcher world, and a man who owns a valuable coursing dog should do well to keep news of the beast's prowess to himself.

21   *An All-round Lurcher*

Lurchers were bred to be all-round hunting dogs, potfillers for country men, providers of both fur and feather and it is doubtful if a lurcher breeder of fifty years ago would have considered using his dog simply for coursing, and even lamping would have seemed a little unusual for the type of lurcher owner described in books such as *It's My Delight*.

Daytime hunting as opposed to coursing with a lurcher is not particularly productive these days, though in times before myxomatosis any lurcher worthy of the name would have justified his keep by simply ranging the fields unattended by its owner, bringing its catch back home as furtively as it could. Not only were rabbits (and just now and again the occasional unwary hare) the sort of quarry these old-fashioned lurchers hunted but pheasants, partridge and even woodcock were struck down by these dogs. At one time an appraisal of a day's qualities in that bible of lurchers, *Exchange and Mart*, would have read 'excellent with fur and feather', but today one rarely sees an advert for a lurcher that refers to its skills in catching feathered game. Far too much attention is paid to the speed of the modern lurcher, its ability to turn a hare or its skill of picking up quarry on the lamp, and because of this shift in values I fear we are losing the real old fashioned all-round hunting dog of old.

To become a daytime hunter of either fur or feather a lurcher must have a nose, and a good one at that. Generally the less sight hound a lurcher has in its makeup, the better the nose, for most greyhounds are strictly coursing or racing dogs and are disinclined to put their noses down to hunt. This is not, as popularly supposed, because the greyhound has a very poor sense of smell, but simply because its eyesight is so efficient, far exceeding the eyesight of other dogs, that this breed prefers to hunt its prey by sight. Greyhounds do in fact often have excellent noses – one obtained by a friend from a flapping track greyhound racer near Redditch had to be seen to be believed and there are few lurchers in that area that can hold a match to her on a scent.

Generally speaking though, few sight hounds use their noses; Salukis are notoriously bad at it, and if they can't see a rabbit or hare they invariably refuse or are unable to hunt it up. Indeed two Salukis

115

owned by a friend of mine, admittedly not a coursing man or someone who uses his dogs for work, have been known to walk past a squatting hare inches from their noses.

Collie bred lurchers are certainly some of the very best of nose workers. E. G. Walsh's famous pair of woolly Norfolk-type lurchers have an excellent reputation as scent hunters, being just as good at hunting up fur as feather. Walsh attributes this good nose to the fact that the dogs have a considerable amount of collie blood in their ancestry, both from their dam and from Lucky, Mick White's famous show lurcher which was said to be a cross between a bearded collie and a deerhound. Terry Aherne's Rusty was famous for his excellent nose and would hunt cover like a spaniel; and some of David Hancock's three-quarter breds are outstanding hunters of rabbits, hare, partridge and pheasant.

Contrary to popular opinion the 'pointing instinct' which involves the dog stopping near to its potential prey raising one foot and pointing in the manner of a setter or a pointer, is not a clear indication that one's lurcher has collie blood. Many lurcher types will perform this feat and I know of a Waterloo Cup cast greyhound that gives a wonderful point when it scents or senses a rabbit in deep cover. I spoke to an Iranian about this pointing instinct which is quite well developed in my own Bedlington/greyhound hybrids, and he remarked that he had seen Saluki type dogs, both in Iran and in Saudi Arabia, perform this feat.

Daytime hunting lurchers, unlike lamping lurchers, should be given every chance to develop their noses and should be taken out as soon as their inoculation assures them of immunity to disease. Allow the puppy to hunt and rummage everywhere. Any experience a puppy gains at this age is priceless, and the more the puppy is taken out, even for rides in a car, the better. There is no substitute for experience and the puppy should see everything the trainer can bring it in contact with. A puppy kept kennelled up and turned loose only on hunting days will not only never become a successful hunter, but will be an absolute nuisance. Such dogs run berserk when taken out, and I don't mean the mad ten minutes most lurchers experience when they are taken hunting. The prisoner, the dog that has not been socialized or allowed to sniff strange scents and run exciting 'lines' across fields, will take a very long time to settle down to a day's hunting.

Starting a dog to rabbit can be done in several ways. The safest, and I mean safest from the owner's point of view, is to take the dog where rabbits abound, if such places still exist these days and allow the dog to make as many tries at a rabbit as it wishes. Disregard the clowns who tell you that their lurcher (which incidentally they have just

'Taffy' working gorse for rabbits

happened to have sold) was catching rabbit by day when it was five months old. Rabbits feeding during the daylight hours rarely stray dangerously far out into the middle of the field and are usually feeding just a few yards from home on or near a well used path that they know inside out. Hence the puppy may run many hundreds of rabbits before it finally connects and picks one up, and the owner should treat the first catch as a red letter day indeed. The newcomer to the lurcher scene must also expect the newly started puppy to make rather a hash of picking up his first rabbit – bowling it, rolling it, trapping it with its paws and in general making one hell of a fool of itself. The owner of the puppy should therefore either brace himself for the jeers and taunts of the onlookers or enter his dog privately when the only person allowed to witness the mess up is himself. Never be disheartened if the puppy takes an aeon of time to make a start and pick up a rabbit – and for Pete's sake don't up and sell the puppy when it makes its first mistake. One of the band of lurchermen who haunt the area where I live, paid £85 for a first cross collie greyhound, a neat long-backed puppy a little too classy to be a half bred in my opinion, but he assured me it was a genuine first cross as he'd seen both the parents. It grew into a rather striking animal, lean and sinewy, lithe and looking like a rather large black whippet. I'm not normally over the moon with smooth-coated dogs as I hunt by night and find a hard coat ideal for inclement weather, but this puppy really was an eye catcher, as attractive a first cross collie greyhound as I've ever seen, with none of the usual stodgy, squat appearance one associates with this first cross. The owner was very proud of his puppy, but he should have known just a little about the cross he had bought and its various faults and failings. When the puppy was six months old he took it out with a crowd of his friends who owned a batch of mongrelly lurchers of no class or breeding and of the sort I wouldn't have said thank you for if they'd offered me one. His puppy ran three, 'muffed' the catches on three and made the boy look a bit of a fool. The lad laughed it off, put on a brave face, but only a blind fool couldn't have seen he was desperately upset about the failure and the ridicule he had received from his associates. I am told that he made two other sorties to try out his puppy and had similar results and three weeks later I saw an ad in *Exchange and Mart* advertising the puppy for sale 'just ready for starting £25'. Just ready for starting the puppy was, and if the fool had taken time he could have made something very useful out of that black puppy.

A year later I visited Lambourn and saw a superb black youngster glowing with health, vitality and just asking for action. In spite of the time that had elapsed since I last saw the puppy I recognized it instantly. After all, it's not often one runs into a classy bitch of that calibre. I was drawn to the chap like a magnet and couldn't wait to ask him about the bitch. He'd bought her from the lad through the advert and taken her out the day after he'd bought her. For three weeks the chap had tried her daily at rabbit, and for three weeks she'd made a fool of herself. Then one day things fell into place. He'd run her at a difficult rabbit that for some reason didn't take the short cut home and made a dash out into the field. She bowled it, rolled it, trapped it with her feet and tried everything but pick it up in her mouth. Finally the rabbit squatted and the bitch picked it up and returned it to hand. After that she never looked back, and all his friends barked up the tale that there wasn't a finer dog in the south at rabbit or hare. I understand she was mated a few weeks ago and the puppies were all booked at £100 a throw, even before they were born.

Contrast this tale with the story of Eddie Jones' Celt, one of the most famous collie three-quarter breds in the country and one E. G. Walsh cannot resist mentioning in his columns in *Shooting News*. I was privileged to receive an invitation to the rather infamous coursing meet which was used for the film *A Hunting Man*. Eddie Jones's Celt was seven months old, and the film shows him as a heavily built puppy, a little ungainly and rather cloddy for a three-quarter bred. A rabbit was ferreted and the warren blocked to prevent the rabbit getting back to ground, and Celt slipped on the rabbit, an easy kill which one of my border terriers would have had no trouble in catching. Celt however had a very bad time with the rabbit and looked an absolute fool, and Eddie's discomfort was made worse by the barracking of the lurcher men watching the fiasco. This sequence however, was seen by 2,000,000 people and Eddie needed to be a strong man not to have quit with the dog. However, the film took ten months to make and by the time it was shown Eddie's dog had become a first class rabbit-catcher and was starting to knock down hares fairly regularly.

A word about ferreting a rabbit for a dog to chase and possibly catch – and I mean a word of warning at that. The public is decidedly anti-coursing and anti-hunting at the time of writing and any action which brings discredit to the sport should be avoided. If a ferret is put to ground, a rabbit bolted and the dog picks up the rabbit, then, providing one had permission to be on the land in pursuit of rabbits, all is well. If, however, the ferret is put to ground, a rabbit bolted, and caught in the nets and then taken out into the middle of the field and released for the dog, then technically the perpetration of the act is an offence under the 1911 Act, the self-same act that saw off the rat pits and was intended to put an end to all forms of baiting. By taking the rabbit into the field, turning it loose and slipping a dog at it, the lurcherman is guilty of baiting the rabbit, and while few police officers are well enough versed in the 1835, 1849 and 1911 Acts, some RSPCA officials are. Even though a prosecution for such an offence may seem unlikely the courts would certainly take a dim view of the whole affair.

Slipping a dog on a tame rabbbit is really asking for trouble and doesn't help to train the dog at all. Most tame rabbits are reluctant to run anyway (so are wild ones if taken off country and released in front of a dog, incidentally), but if one is discovered encouraging the dog to kill a tame rabbit the courts and the general public alike get greatly offended. The Tamworth case of 1983 can illustrate my point. A Tamworth-based lurcherman, new to the game, but owning two lurchers and several greyhounds, owned a tame rabbit that he decided to kill and eat. Instead of delivering a quick rabbit punch and finishing the business immediately, he put the rabbit down for his lurcher which chased and terrified the poor creature. Neighbours reported the owner of the rabbit and lurcher and the courts dished out a stinging fine. Needless to say the newspapers really went to town about the story and gave field sports generally a very bad write up. As hunters we are under attack from the public most of the time, and we should be doing everything to protect our sport, not leave it open to attack.

After a while a dog which is rabbited regularly develops a very efficient style of rabbiting and an individualistic style at that, for no two dogs use the same technique. The walking-up on rabbits, freezing to stillness whenever a rabbit raises an ear and prepares to run, is a technique many lurchers seem to learn. Most lurcher books state that this method of hunting is a clear indication of collie blood in a lurcher, but this just isn't so. This method of hunting is a quality most pure bred sighthounds learn, and many longdogs develop this method of stalking to a fine degree. Trixie, a genuine deerhound/greyhound bred by Cider Mills Kennels, Gwent, specialists in producing lurchers and particularly longdogs, was perhaps the finest exponent of the art of walking up quarry before making a try at it, that I have seen. This longdog, a good quality, brindled, long-haired bitch had the advantage of being very tall and thus able to see a considerable distance. When she saw a rabbit out feeding, she did a quick spot of mental arithmetic and decided whether or not the rabbit was too close to the hedge or the warren to try. If she considered the rabbit worthy of her attentions she would walk slowly towards it, stopping and freezing whenever the rabbit looked up and when she was within striking distance she made her bid, and it was surprising how such a large dog managed to snatch up rabbits which were racing for home.

Another excellent walker up of rabbits, as good a catch dog as

Evans' Trixie, was Barnard's Mick, a Linden Eland bred dog which has sired more show-winning lurchers than any modern stud greyhound; for unlike Eland, Mick was a handsome dog who passed on his type, staying power and courage to his progeny and bred many of the three-quarter bred deerhound longdogs in and around the Lambourn district. Mick mastered this walking up technique immediately he retired from coursing, and within weeks he was working rabbits like a veteran. This dog died last year and he will be sadly missed by those breeders who used him, for unlike most other lurcher breeders I believe the greyhound side of the pedigree of a lurcher to be even more important than the non-sighthound side. Certainly many of the lurchers Barnard's dog sired inherited this dog's walking up instinct, as well as his nose, for many of Linden Eland's puppies have excellent noses, though this is a quality to which breeders of coursing greyhounds pay very little attention. Barnard's dog sired some fifty-five puppies, primarily to half-bred deerhounds of known breeding, and made a considerable impact on the longdog scene.

Lurchers sometimes work cover as well as spaniels, though I know of no way a cover shy dog can be forced to enter thorns unless it wants to, and coat has nothing to do with this reluctance to enter nettles and brambles. In fact one of the best cover-working lurchers I know has a coat as fine as a whippet, yet will crash though cover. Spider, owned by Phil Riley of Nottingham, was bought as a puppy from Moses Smith of Etwall, Derby; he was bred from a rather nondescript bitch called Penguin, put to Terry Aherne's dog. Spider was outstanding in cover and a grand catch dog in tight places. Smith considers this litter to be the best Penguin ever bred, though she was a prolific bitch and died at the age of seventeen. Her puppies when she was mated to a collie-bred sire were outstanding, though many were cloddy and unsightly. When mated to deerhound-bred stock, she produced some really good lookers which were indifferent workers and failed to respond to training. I had one of these deerhoundy hybrids bred from Penguin sent to me for training. The dog was a startling looking beast, a tall brindled rough coated lurcher and a real show stopper. As a lamper it was indifferent, as a hunter its nose was not satisfactory and its coursing qualities were nothing to shout about, yet its half-brothers sired by a variety of collie hybrids were wonderful all-round hunters and versatile as labradors.

Working cover, or rather working a rabbit out of cover, is an art some lurchers acquire and when learning this art they are a pleasure to watch. Dogs which crash straight into cover like terriers usually only succeed in bolting the rabbit, which ninety-nine times out of a hundred escapes. Smart lurchers make gentle 'puts' at the cover, darting round the bushes at the first sign of movement, and these are the lurchers for picking up rabbits in cover. Few longdogs ever acquire these skills, and are really more at home on open fields than pushing rabbits out of bushes, and the most efficient dogs for working woodland for fur or feather are rarely above 23 inches at the shoulder. Harold Hodson Walker of Tutbury has produced some excellent dogs for woodland work using a collie-bred stud dog on tracking greyhound bitches, and generally speaking collie-bred lurchers seem at their best under these conditions, though Don Bakewell's Bedlington hybrids, both Bedlington greyhound and Bedlington whippet crosses have an excellent reputation for working in deep cover.

My column in *Shooting News* nets a fairly regular bag of letters concerning lurchers and one of the most common questions put to me is how a trainer can encourage a dog to work feather as well as fur. D. B. Plummer in *Merle* writes that some dogs are naturally inclined to take feather and gypsies did at one time breed a type of lurcher called a 'kanniechor' or stealer of chickens. Some strains of lurcher are very enthusiastic about catching feather, while others are particularly suspicious of even picking up a dead bird. Collie-blooded lurchers containing at least a quarter part collie are perhaps the best of catch dogs for feather. Aherne tells of a dog he obtained in lieu of a fee when a blue greyhound bitch was mated to Rusty. Aherne chose a black smooth-coated male puppy for his fee and sold it to a young lurcherman in Chester. The dog became a good rabbit and hare dog, but an outstanding bird-catcher and crowned an outstanding career on feather by taking a Canada Goose in full plumage (geese are relatively easy to take during the moult). Sadly the dog was killed through a car accident before the end of its second year, or it might have become an all time great lurcher.

Most dogs can be fairly easily started to feather if trained to bird catching as puppies. Training on a furry dummy attached to a lead is usually a good way to start a dog to rabbit. Likewise a dead bird used for retrieving lessons or tied to a leash and pulled along in front of a puppy will usually do the trick in starting a puppy's interest in feather. Personally I would prefer to start a puppy on a dead pheasant or partridge; a road casualty will do as I find lurchers are reluctant to pick up crows, doves or pigeons during their initial training, though they soon take to this sort of quarry later.

Pheasant and partridge taking, however, is quite a distinct art from simply hunting these birds up and the lurcher will miss a great number of game birds before it finally connects and brings one down. Pheasant explode from the ground or cover noisily with a great deal of commotion while partridge whirr upwards with a sound which is characteristic of their species. Both these methods of getting on the wing are deliberately noisy, for such a noise unnerves a predator for a split second which enables the bird to get away. My present male lurcher, a gutsy little dog with bags of spirit, will take both partridge and pheasant with some degree of success. However, on his first encounter with partridge exploding from the grass, he turned tail and ran back behind me and it was six months before he would come up on one, cause it to fly and go up after the whirring bird. When pheasants or partridge fly off, don't discourage the dog from chasing them, however fruitless the chase may be. In fact a dog should be urged to chase a low-flying pheasant.

A few handfuls of grain flung near a pheasant shoot will usually entice birds off their normal habitat and allow a lurcher at least a chance of catching them. Likewise a garden with a patch of artichokes will also bring them in. Of course, the lurchermen will be decidedly unpopular if he entices pheasants or other game on to his land and takes them with a lurcher, but then I doubt whether lurchermen are out to win popularity polls anyway.

Perhaps the best way to start one's lurcher to partridge or pheasant or even grouse (if the lurcherman has access to these evershrinking grouse moors) is to follow on after a shoot. Very few shooting men, particularly hunters of game birds admit to ever leaving wounded birds around after a shoot, but a trip around with a good lurcher with a fine nose will prove otherwise and picking up badly wounded birds is not actually harming a shoot providing the lurcher owner stays on the property where he has permission. A reliable lurcher will pick up quite a few runners which Labrador retrievers and spaniels have missed, and it is surprising how far strong runners will stray unless the district is thick with foxes which usually take full advantage of the damaged birds left behind after a shoot. Boothby (for all his seedy appearance) was often invited on shoots where after receiving his 15/– and touching his cap, he would depart, pick up his lurcher and that evening would offer Dad a selection ranging from snipe to wild goose. Some of Boothby's other little tricks concerning the taking of game were less pleasant, and would have brought the RSPCA banging on his door if they had known about them, but that is a different story.

A daytime lurcher may not bring down the quantity of game a lamping dog will catch, but there is a definite pleasure in working dogs by day, watching them hunt up, panic rabbits out of bushes and pluck pheasants from the air, and this pleasure is not experienced by a man who hunts exclusively with lamping dogs.

22 *Lurcher Breeding*

At the time of writing, let's make no bones about it, lurcher breeding is big business. A top grade puppy will fetch £80–£100 and trained dogs up to a thousand pounds, though for some inexplicable reason lamping dogs fetch far less than a dog whose only skill is that it can course and bring down a hare. However, for an equally inexplicable reason, puppies bred exclusively for coursing, that is Saluki-bred longdogs or the ubiquitous deerhound hybrid are fetching less than the collie-bred lurchers, which are the only true all-round lurchers.

Many dog breeders are now producing lurchers for a living, but breeding for profit is frowned on by many coursing men. Providing the professional breeder does his best to improve on the lurchers already in existence, and breeds first rate, well-reared puppies which in the right hands will do the job for which they are intended, he is certainly not doing any disservice to the world of lurchers. If one breeds the right stuff, starting from known pedigrees, then a good profit can be made breeding lurcher puppies. If one buys in rubbish of dubious pedigree, mates it to dogs of equally mixed and unknown background, and sells the puppies with a fictitious pedigree then the chances are your first litter will sell exceedingly well; but word gets around that one is breeding rubbish and future litters (even if one decides to breed top-grade puppies) will be a lot more difficult to dispose of even at give-away prices. There is only one type of lurcher to breed, and that is the best.

On the other hand, many people are not particularly interested in breeding puppies for money, for having found that a tried and trusted bitch, a bitch which has put in years of hard work and has been an absolute treasure is getting old, they decide to perpetuate a first rate bloodline by breeding from that bitch. Puppies from such bitches may well find homes with friends rather than being offered for sale, but once again I must repeat the old adage that there is only one type of stock worth breeding, and that is the best.

Therefore before considering the commercial aspects of breeding a litter to sell, let us examine the position of the man who wishes to perpetrate the line from a tried and tested bitch. Firstly, the breeder must take stock of the lurchers he is keeping, and must steel himself to stop that most destructive genetic programme, namely 'kennel blindness' – a common affliction of lurchermen who consider that their perfect lurcher is flawless and excellent in every way and it is impossible to improve on this bloodline. The perfect lurcher has yet to be born. So the lurcherman who decides to breed from a good bitch should draw up a list of a bitch's good points (and also a list of some of the qualities that may be lacking) and find a dog which excels in the points in which his bitch is weak; but above all he must find a dog whose pedigree is known, for the majority of lurchers offered for sale are such a hotch potch of breeds thrown together by well meaning amateur breeders that only dogs whose breeding can be verified by their owners should be mated to the potential brood bitch. Avoid the use of 'bitza' dogs, dogs with bits of this breed and bits of that, no matter how well they perform on the field; for mating such a dog to what is probably an equally mongrelly bitch will produce such a variable litter that there is literally no guarantee how the puppies will turn out. E. G. Walsh's advice in *Lurchers and Longdogs* – have a lurcher which is a hybrid of as few breeds as possible – is excellent.

So how does one correct the faults of one's bitch to breed a puppy dog which will grow up to be a better lurcher than the dam? Firstly, let us assume that the would-be breeder's bitch has an excellent nose, great stamina and wonderful tractability, and add to this the almost instinctive ability to be able to predict the ways of rabbits and hares. But she is just a shade short in speed with not enough thrust and poke about her to come up on hare. What her puppies therefore need is just a little more speed, so the obvious choice of dog as a mate for this bitch to give her puppies the extra speed is a sight hound – a greyhound, a Borzoi, a Saluki, an Afghan hound or deerhound – and mating one's bitch to a sight hound would literally guarantee that the puppies will be a whole lot faster than the dam. But wait a moment: a cross with a sight hound will certainly give your strain of lurcher speed, yet on the other hand a whole lot of other qualities will suffer if one mates the lurcher to a greyhound. Pattinson in *Coursing* suggests that a cross with a greyhound is necessary to prevent what he calls 'reversion' or the lurcher strain becoming cloddy and shapeless and possibly losing a little of the quality coursing men call 'thrust' – instant take-off speed and the ability to get into top gear in just a few yards. For all his experience of lurcher breeding he is quite wrong, for a cross with a greyhound has a devastating effect on the all-round working ability of a lurcher type and a cross with a Saluki literally annuls all tractability in a strain of lurcher. Greyhounds (and most other sight hounds) must rank as the most unintelligent of all breeds of dog. Hence greyhound blood is ameliorated with collie blood to produce an all-round hunting dog. Now by definition, lurchers have a fair proportion of greyhound blood in their ancestry so a massive infusion is not only likely to produce a somewhat faster dog but also a less tractable dog, a dog with less hunting instinct (as opposed to coursing instinct) and a dog with considerably less stamina, for greyhounds are seldom asked to run long distances on the track or on the coursing field.

What therefore should the potential breeder mate to his lurcher to produce a better all round hunting dog? Well the simple answer is a better all-round hunting lurcher with the same speed, instinct, tractability and nose, but greater speed and thrust. Looking for such a dog will take time, but it is far better to seek out such a dog than chance the litter wastage one expects when one mates two lurchers of dubious mixed ancestry together. I interviewed David Hancock who has a great many dogs at stud both to lurchers and greyhounds. Hancock advises mating very fleet three-quarter bred collie greyhound studs to bitches which lack speed and advises against using half-bred collie greyhounds (which would create too great a litter wastage when mated to a somewhat heavy nondescript lurcher) and he certainly advises against mating such a lurcher to a greyhound or other sighthound.

D. B. Plummer, in his private diary notes for 1967, writes that he owned a heavily built but useful and bright lurcher bitch during that year and in order to perpetuate the lines decided to mate her to a greyhound. The resultant puppies were fast, game and (judging from photographs) show stoppers. Plummer put them out to friends who tried and tested them to the full. Apart from great speed, which made the puppies satisfactory, if not great, hare killers, they had little else to recommend them.

Fast, but rather brainless strains of lurchers of nondescript breeding, more akin to longdogs than lurchers, can be improved by mating to collie-bred studs rather than pure-bred collies. Crossing with collies produces an enormous litter wastage though it has been known to throw up the occasional world beater. David Hancock tells me that he gets several of these longdog bitches brought to stud by lurchermen who are unhappy about the intractable nature of their longdog types. Most opt to mate their bitches to three-quarter bred collie greyhounds, but Hancock does not consider that mating infuses enough brain and instinct into a strain of running dog which is predominantly greyhound. He usually advises these longdog breeders to mate their bitches to lightly built half-bred collie greyhound studs to give added brain, nose and stamina to the crossbred.

The reduction of size in the progeny of a beloved bitch is a point one must discuss now that the huge deerhound greyhound hybrid 28–29-

inch giants, which were popular during the post-Lambourn boom, are now falling out of fashion. At the time of writing 25-inch dogs and 24-inch bitches are in vogue and breeders who intend to sell their surplus progeny should endeavour to produce stock of this size. Mating a towering giant of a deerhound-bred longdog to a whippet – a very popular mating as advertisements in *Exchange and Mart* seem to indicate – will not produce the desired results, however. The progeny of the mating rarely grows into the mean size between the sizes of sire and dam but turn out to be very variable litters indeed, ranging from 17 inch whippety stock to 28-inch giants. Reduction in size is only achieved by mating one's oversized bitch to a dog of the desired size and keeping back an average-sized puppy from the litter.

The same applies in reverse to tiny undersized lurchers, and it is amazing how popular under 22-inch lurchers are at present, though it is doubtful if these lurchers are superior in every way to a good class coursing bred whippet. To breed a dog or bitch puppy of the desired size from such a tiny lurcher, it is not good policy to mate such a bitch to a giant dog but rather to a dog of the size one desires.

A number of professional lurcher breeders have started up in business since the Lambourn Lurcher Show triggered off a renewed interest in lurchers. Breeders who specialize in various crosses, be they deerhound/greyhound, the ubiquitous Saluki/greyhound, Bedlington terrier/greyhound, or the now very popular collie hybrids, are more likely to succeed in business than the dabbler who breeds from bitches of unknown pedigree puppies which are sold to unsuspecting suckers as whatever cross they are seeking.

Greyhounds for lurcher breeding are easily obtainable at present, though there are I believe moves afoot in the NGRA to prevent the surplus or track damaged bitches finishing up in the hands of people who might misuse and mistreat them – and make no bones about it, some cast greyhounds finish their days in very bad places indeed. I must repeat that, contrary to popular opinion, not every greyhound is suitable for breeding top-grade lurchers and the would-be lurcher breeder would do better to politely give offers of flapping track bred greyhounds a miss and get in contact with a breeder of coursing greyhounds to request a bitch who is past her time as a coursing prospect.

A few years ago I would have considered using any track greyhound as a base for breeding lurchers, and my first lurchers were in fact bred from a track greyhound which had run at licensed tracks and won well until her fifth year. These days however taller, stronger greyhounds are appearing on the coursing scene, possibly due to a breeding programme to compensate for the slight change in the rules con-

Centre: Linden Elan breed coursing greyhound
Right: Border and bearded collie
Left: the result of mating a collie greyhound to a greyhound: a rough-coated
first-cross lurcher

cerning the awarding of points during competitive coursing, and these tall, powerfully built coursing dogs seem to be better suited to the production of lurchers. This however is not everyone's opinion, and one lurcher breeder who wrote to me after my articles on lurcher breeding had appeared in the sporting press said that he would not consider using coursing bred greyhounds to breed his lurchers, as they lacked the initial speed and dash of a well-bred track greyhound. Most renowned lurcher breeders are particularly choosy about the greyhounds they use to create their strains. Don Bakewell used only the tallest track greyhounds to compensate for the lack of size of his Bedlington terrier while Aubrey Fryer is particularly careful about his choice of coursing greyhound dams and sires. E. G. Walsh used coursing greyhound blood in the creation of his strain and at Lowther

Show in 1983 remarked on some of the large exhibits, wondering what dreadful cast greyhounds were used in their creation. David Hancock uses coursing greyhounds for preference and Irish bred dogs whenever he can get them, even if it means going to Ireland – though Timmy, his most photographed three-quarter bred collie/greyhound hybrid was bred from a track greyhound, as was Vermeuil of Staffords dun, merle, wall-eyed, three quarter bred. Each year sees bigger and better coursing greyhounds available, and, though the end of competitive coursing is on the horizon, the lurcher breeder should avail himself of the best possible coursing lines before these go the way of the dodo.

As to the dogs to be mated to the greyhounds to produce lurchers, care should be taken in their selection. For those who favour the very popular Saluki/greyhound longdog an excellent mix can be produced by contacting a Saluki coursing club representative, and, providing the breeder is willing to mate a good quality stud dog to a greyhound, this type of dog would obviously be preferable to the show dogs bred from many generations of dogs that have never seen a hare. Coursing Saluki breeders are as a rule not unwilling to mate their dogs to greyhound to produce longdogs, but many breeders of deerhounds are decidedly antipathetic about allowing their stud dogs to serve greyhounds. Shortly after my attack on this deerhound/greyhound hybrid in the pages of *Shooting News* in 1983, an article in which I described the shortcomings of the modern show deerhound, the writer of the breed columns in two leading dog magazines wrote that he was glad that such an article appeared principally because deerhound breeders would no longer be inundated with owners of greyhounds and lurchers requesting the use of stud dogs to breed tall longdogs for coursing.

Regarding the use of collies to breed the now very popular collie greyhound hybrid which may perpetrate its lines further in the popular three-quarter bred stock, the collie used should be tall, far taller than the type used on the hills of Central Wales. Few first crosses are capable of hare taking, but one *Shooting News* reader who wrote to me concerning this type of lurcher says that he has seen 25-inch collies on Exmoor, long lanky dogs, ideally suited to lurcher breeding. David Hancock believes that a more practicable type of collie to use is a mix of bearded and border collie, taller than the typical border collie and fuller coated, for protection against thorns but still having border collie tractability. Actually any working bearded collie would be just as useful, as working lines are becoming so rare in beardies that the majority of breeders have introduced border collie blood into their beardies to prevent peculiarities which result from inbreeding. However, many of these breeders of working bearded collies are shepherds living in the remote areas of Scotland, who jealously guard their strains of sheepdog and are more than reluctant to use their studs on greyhound bitches, no matter how high the stud fee offered. Once more it is necessary to quote David Hancock, an authority on this type of hybrid:

> Few breeders of working bearded collies were even prepared to listen to my request to mate a greyhound bitch to tried and tested working bearded collies. Hence it became necessary to buy one, and the only breeder of these dogs I considered was breeding exactly the type of dogs I wanted, lived in the Pentland Hills and bred a long-legged shaggy-coated strain which he sheared each year at shearing time along with his sheep. I keep two studs, a bearded/border blend and a Pentland-bred beardie for out crossing.

However whether one intends to breed lurcher to lurcher, longdog to longdog or simply create a strain of lurcher by mating non-sighthound blooded dogs to greyhounds, the mating process, conception, pregnancy and parturition is essentially the same – though some track bred greyhounds are often very difficult to mate.

Most strains of longdogs or lurchers with a high percentage of sight hound blood in their ancestry rarely come in season more than once a year and the reason for this biological peculiarity is obvious if one examines the rules of greyhound racing, which, while they were drawn up only a matter of sixty years ago (1926 to be exact), may have altered the breeding cycle of greyhounds dramatically. Racing regulations decree that in-season bitches are not allowed to race on licensed tracks for some time before the bitch comes into season and for some six weeks after season as in-season bitches not only distract dogs, but also develop a layer of fatty tissue around their hearts which considerably affects the bitch's track performance, and can also seriously damage a bitch if she puts in a strenuous effort at the clockwork hare. Therefore track bitches which come in season twice a year are barred from competing on tracks for considerable periods of time and are not favoured by racing greyhound owners. Hence a 'once a year' greyhound strain may have been developed since 1926. D. B. Plummer, however, in articles published in scientific periodicals, states that he believes greyhounds are naturally inclined to come in season just once a year and that the track racing regulations have altered the oestral cycle of greyhounds little if at all.

Bitches normally stand for mating during the twelfth day of season, though some may reach sexual readiness earlier or later, and a much surer indication of a bitch's readiness to accept a dog is when the breeder notices that the bitch turns her tail aside and pushes her vulva towards an interested dog or bitch. A bitch will then show little or no bloody discharge from the vagina and in this condition will not only tolerate the attentions of a dog, but will usually conceive when mated. My first greyhound became extraordinarily excited when near readiness and not only bit through the wires of her pen to get to an adult dog but barked non-stop from the tenth to the sixteenth day of season. In fact her incessant barking gave an indication that she was ready to mate, and the Bedlington terrier stud dog who lived four doors away from our house and who mated her every other season throughout her life also set up a cacophony of noise around the time my greyhound was in season. On the subject of mating a bitch to the same dog time and time again there is a curious superstition among greyhound men concerning this practice. Many greyhound breeders believe that if a bitch is repeatedly mated to the same dog time and time again, the puppies become progressively weaker and weaker in successive litters. This theory, known as 'saturation' in greyhound racing parlance, is certainly not borne out by fact – Beef Cutlet produced champions in each and every litter he sired to Lady Eleanor so there is no reason why a dog should not mate the same bitch time and time again if the results of previous litters are satisfactory. Saturation, like telegony, is yet another ridiculous superstition which is the plague of sensible scientific dog breeding.

Trained stud dogs, particularly stud dogs required to mate bitches very much larger than themselves, are treasures and are worth considerably more than their weight in gold. In order to mate taller bitches the stud dog has to have an excellent working relationship with his owner. Small dogs need to either be lifted to mate a bitch or be allowed to stand on a platform to perform – an action which looks decidedly strange, but is essential if a small dog is to be mated to a big bitch. Some years ago I took a well-bred track greyhound, a whopper of 26 inches – very big indeed for a track dog – to be mated by a Bedlington terrier dog owned by Michael Bevins. The Bedlington was a grim and determined little scrapper, as game a terrier as I've ever seen, bred down from Newcombe's Rillington strain. I'd seen Bevin's dog work badger – it was legal then – and also fetch shot game to hand, perhaps not as well as a spaniel, but good enough for any terrier. Furthermore he was a dog that would nail rabbits in a hedgerow as well as any whippet. He was just the dog I wanted to mate, to breed the sort of lurcher I value most. That week a flapping track man 'weighed' in a quantity of brass trimmings at the yard and mentioned he'd a track bitch he was giving away because she'd come in season and was over the top for racing anyway. I hurried across to

Bevin's house and asked to mate her, but was dismayed when I saw the disparity in size between the Bedlington and greyhound. Bevin wasn't perplexed at all and I could see why. His dog had served a great number of greyhounds and knew the problems involved: the dog leaped on a child's chair and waited for the greyhound to be moved to him. There was a sad ending to the tale, however, as the bitch didn't take.

Not all dogs will mate as easily. Some dogs object to being touched during the mating process, while others will not mate at all if the owner of the bitch stands behind them. This sort of behaviour is usually the result of inexperience and as soon as a dog sorts out his little sexual hang-ups he usually tends to co-operate more fully.

I don't own a stud dog, that is I don't offer a dog at public stud, mainly because I don't have the time to fool around with a dog mating bitches but primarily because there are some fairly seedy people in the lurcher world and I don't encourage them to come to my house. However most owners of stud dogs refuse to allow a bitch to be served by a dog unless she is muzzled and one has only to see the damage done to an inexperienced stud dog or to the owner by a greyhound bitch to see why. Teddy Moritz of New Jersey bought a large three-quarter bred collie greyhound from Joan Hancock and Joan's account of the mating which produced this bitch is worthy of relating. Joan had bought a very well bred coursing bitch, a good bitch for coming up on hare, but a devil with other dogs running with her. She was also death on any other terrier which strayed too near her and this boded evil for any dog which tried to mate her. Joan mated her to D. B. Plummer's stud dog, Merle, but as the dog penetrated the bitch she struck out at him, missing him but biting Plummer through the arm to the bone. She locked her teeth like a bull terrier and refused to release the hold until choked off. After that she was muzzled, and muzzled securely every time she was mated.

If a bitch stands easily to be mated, without snapping, showing aggression to the stud or tucking her tail between her legs, then one mating is probably enough. If she is a bit hesitant or screams like a stuck pig while mating, another visit to the stud dog is called for. If after the second mating she continues to stand for several days a third mating, if the owner of the stud is willing, is on the cards for the chances are the bitch has not conceived to the dog during the first two matings. I'm not sure whether the persistent matings advised in *The Complete Lurcher* are necessary, but repeated mating certainly does no harm and professional lurcher breeders usually mate their greyhounds as often as they will stand, if the dog is not needed for visiting bitches.

At about the fifth week after mating, a bitch will begin to show signs that she has conceived, and personally in spite of the number of experts I meet who believe they can tell whether or not a bitch is pregnant before this time, I think it is highly unlikely that they can. I spoke to my vet about this and he also said that he would be hard put to make anything more than an educated guess as to whether or not a bitch had 'taken' before the fifth week after mating.

As soon as the bitch begins to show signs of pregnancy the owner should steel himself and reject invitations to come coursing or particularly lamping with the bitch. There are tales of the dam of a Waterloo Cup winner which coursed and killed a fox a day before she whelped her champion puppy. However, for every happy ending I've heard regarding the coursing of a pregnant bitch, I can relate four desperately sad stories. One such account reached me just the other day from a country man called Carl Pollitt from Doncaster who spent a great deal of time mating his greyhound to a top class lurcher dog but allowed the bitch a lengthy and arduous course during the sixth week of her pregnancy. The bitch miscarried a week later and passed a litter of very dead puppies.

The bitch's food should also be increased after the fifth week of pregnancy – not dramatically or else the bitch may become too obese to pass her puppies – but a gradual increase is necessary to get the best results from the litter about to be born. I give an egg or so a day from the fifth week in addition to the bitch's normal diet and pack her full of as much flesh as possible from the sixth week onwards. I don't like dog meat for pregnant bitches as the mix gives bulk, but simply does not give the necessary protein and vitamins a bitch needs to produce a healthy litter. Meal fed bitches are usually a bit fleshless after parturition and this condition worsens rather than improves as time goes on. Remember that as pregnancy proceeds the contents of the abdomen get larger and restrict the size of the stomach. Hence a food of a more concentrated nature is called for – and meat, not meal, is the most concentrated food available for a carnivore. Dogs are not usually fussy creatures and greyhounds and lurchers certainly aren't. Hence any form of butcher's waste, even lights, if one is pushed, will do. I have fed waste sausage meat, unsaleable black pudding, fatty snaps of breast of mutton and even meat that was so putrid that travellers remarked on the smell of my vehicle, and have had no problems at all breeding and rearing puppies on such a mix.

Lurchers are usually very easy to whelp, far easier than most breeds of dog in fact, for not only are the heads of lurcher and other sight hound puppies unlikely to jam in the birth canal, but lurchers are usually lean, easily conditioned and superbly fit; and in such condition they rarely if ever need help in whelping. Just now and again a bitch does get trouble whelping with a puppy jamming, or a womb so tired that it refuses to contract to expel the puppy. My advice is, in these circumstances, to get professional help immediately. Get the vet around as soon as possible and the chances are you'll save both dam and puppies. Playing around trying to extract a puppy by hand (if the breeder is an amateur) or getting in an equally unknowledgeable friend, is inviting trouble and wasting valuable time. Greyhounds, sight hounds, longdogs and lurchers are tough creatures, but even dogs as hardy as these are not indestructible. Look at it this way: one puppy saved will pay a vet's bill twice over and a stingy attitude hardly goes hand in hand with a successful dog breeder anyway.

The chances are you'll arrive home from work one day and find the litter born, cleaned, dried and suckling, and providing your shed or spare room is warm you'll have no further trouble with your litter until time for weaning draws nigh. Take off any dew claws on the puppies' legs, front and rear, though few lurches are born with rear dew claws. Dew claws left on are nuisances and, as the dog gets older and starts coursing these claws are a source of trouble. They invariably tangle in long grass, bleed copiously, get knocked off and bleed even more copiously, and are such a nuisance that it is difficult to understand why a dog still has these claws, for they serve no useful purpose. Some advise leaving dew claws on, as they are supposed to help the dog to climb rugged places, but, for the life of me, I can't see how these claws can help a dog in any way at all. Cut them off with curved scissors when the puppies are two days old; it won't hurt the puppies much, and, providing you've seen someone do this dew claw removing just once, it's an easy task.

Puppies need to be kept warm to grow well and a sunny room in a house is ideal. If this is not available a draughtproof shed is useful; but for the first few days of a puppy's life it needs heat, so unless there is a heatwave raging outside, put a piglamp over the puppies for just a few days. It will cost very little more than an electric light bulb to run and the difference it makes to the whelps will pay for the lamp bulb and electricity time and time again. Remember that a good puppy well reared and properly fed will give maybe twelve years' service and pay for its keep many times over. A badly reared puppy reared in cold conditions will never be anything but second rate, no matter how well it is trained and how often it is worked. Travellers rarely breed lurchers in the winter time for a traveller's lurcher must whelp beneath a caravan in harsh conditions, and over the years itinerants have realized that warmth is necessary for puppy rearing. Hence only summer bred puppies are produced by gypsies and tinkers.

At about three weeks of age puppies start to take an interest in food.

Puppies which avidly suck at meat before they are fourteen days old need watching for the chances are that puppies of this age showing an interest in solid food are not getting enough milk from the bitch. Three weeks after the birth of her puppies the bitch's flow of milk is becoming less, so puppies must look elsewhere for sustenance. Raw and bloody flesh is the food to give whelps of this age, meat still on the bone which the puppies will suck at and eventually tear and swallow. Some bitches deliberately bolt great quantities of meat and vomit it back to feed the whelps and though the sight of a litter of puppies paddling in an evil-smelling pool of vomit may look disgusting, it is the bitch's way of shredding and partly digesting food for her puppies to eat. Meal-fed bitches usually produce some very evil-smelling mounds of partly digested food and if this is not cleaned up after the puppies have eaten their fill it decomposes and starts off all manner of illnesses in the litter, particularly gastritis and various forms of enteritis.

Allow weaning puppies as much flesh as they will eat, and feed five or six times a day if possible. Some bitches will allow their whelps to gorge at the food bowl and refuse to eat until the puppies have had enough. Others can be very jealous about food and menace and snap at the puppies if they try to feed in the presence of the bitch. These puppies should be fed separately and the bitch kept well away at feeding times. The late Ted Adsett, a well known terrier breeder, used to tell a tale of a lurcher keeper he knew well. This man had reared a lovely litter from his straw-coloured Norfolk bitch mated to a similar type of dog. At three weeks old the puppies looked a picture, but Adsett noticed that as the pups crawled near the food tray the bitch grew anxious and began to growl softly. Adsett warned the owner of the lurcher, but like most young lads the youth knew it all and refused to heed Old Ted. One day the youth opened the shed to water the litter and found his bitch guarding a cow's head in the corner growling and menacing over it while around the pen her puppies lay bitten and with necks broken. Sudden deaths in hitherto healthy litters may also be worth watching, particularly if the dead puppy was the most forward and advanced whelp in the litter. The chances are the puppy was a little too forward for its own good and failed to heed a warning the bitch gave as it approached the food tray. For these reasons I take the bitch out when I feed the puppies and replace her only when they have obviously had all they can manage. Bitches also get decidedly touchy about the puppies suckling her when the whelps have developed their first teeth, for the suckling action then causes the teats to become raw, cracked and inflamed and thus sore to the touch. For this reason it is good sense to move a bitch from her puppies for several hours a day when the puppies are five or six weeks old. A relative of mine in Grasmere once reared a litter of hound puppies for a Lakeland hunt and all went well until the puppies were six weeks old and the bitch couldn't get away from them. She became sore and began to snap at the puppies, killing three of her own litter.

Puppies should be sold at eight weeks of age and not before. At this age they take the shock of leaving their dams for a new home well and while breeders may be encouraged to tempt the buyer to take a puppy before this – for puppies of eight weeks of age will eat a breeder out of house and home – it is far better to wait two more weeks before selling. Admittedly, I've bought puppies of five weeks old and reared them, but a great many puppies purchased at this age, particularly in winter time, come to grief.

Selling lurchers is good fun if one has patience, for an advert in *Exchange and Mart* attracts a whole horde of buyers, some genuine, the others with nothing better to do than to spend a few hours looking at puppies. Many adverts read 'No time wasters please', and this gives some indication of the clientele such an advertisement can attract. If the stock you have for sale is well bred and equally well reared, then by all means ask a good price and state the price in the advertisement. This might deter some time wasters, but likewise might attract even more. Believe me, there are some amazing people in the lurcher world. Expect a strange selection of phone calls ranging from idiots who want to challenge your bitch to a coursing contest to those who treat the vendor of lurchers as just someone to talk to – rather like a desperate man gets in contact with the Samaritans. I find it very hard to be polite to such fools, but if one needs to sell lurcher puppies one needs to be firm but polite. John Kearsley, who until last year specialized in deerhound/greyhound hybrids, tells some amazing tales of idiots who phoned him at all hours of the night. Some offered to swop him lurchers for his puppies; others wanted to trade 'spoiled' terrier puppies ruined by premature entering, while one or two requested he arranged hire purchase on the puppies!

The majority of his potential purchasers haggled, and were almost hurt when Kearsley stuck to his original price. Some even asked for written guarantees on the puppies with written promises that Kearsley would take the puppies back if they weren't catching at six months old. Others asked for eight week old puppies on trial. Eventually Kearsley was stuck with one exceptionally fine litter of deerhound X greyhounds, bred from a really good deerhound and a top class greyhound bitch, and was beset with hagglers. Kearsley refused to lower his price and eventually put the litter down. When I asked him why he gave up breeding this elegant line he replied that since he ceased to breed lurchers, 'I am no longer plagued by idiots.'

Some buyers are genuine, however, and providing you are selling the right type of stock, you will make some good friends by breeding lurchers. Not all the lurcher fraternity are idiots – though sometimes it seems as though the majority are!